Total Life
Prosperity

Total Life Prosperity

14 PRACTICAL STEPS TO RECEIVING GOD'S FULL BLESSING

CREFLO A. DOLLAR JR.

THOMAS NELSON PUBLISHERS®
Nashville

Published in Nashville, Tennessee, by Thomas Nelson, Inc.

Unless otherwise noted, Scripture quotations are from THE KING JAMES VERSION of the Bible.

Scripture quotations noted NKJV are from THE NEW KING JAMES VERSION. Copyright © 1979, 1980, 1982, Thomas Nelson, Inc., Publishers.

Scripture quotations noted AMPLIFIED are from THE AMPLIFIED BIBLE: Old Testament. Copyright © 1962, 1964 by Zondervan Publishing House (used by permission); and from THE AMPLIFIED NEW TESTAMENT. Copyright © 1958 by the Lockman Foundation (used by permission).

Scripture quotations noted *The Message* are from *The Message: The New Testament in Contemporary English*. Copyright © 1993 by Eugene H. Peterson.

Scripture quotations noted TLB are from *The Living Bible*, copyright 1971 by Tyndale House Publishers, Wheaton, IL. Used by permission.

Library of Congress Cataloging-in-Publication Data

Dollar, Creflo A.
    Total life prosperity : 14 practical steps to receiving God's full blessing / Creflo A. Dollar Jr.
        p.   cm.
    ISBN 0-7852-6900-2 (pbk.)
    1. Success—Religious aspects—Christianity. 2. Wealth—Religious aspects—Christianity.   I. Title.
    BV4598.3.D65 1999
    248.4—dc21   99-15324
                                                                            CIP

Printed in the United States of America.

7 8 9 10 PHX 04 03 02 01

CONTENTS

CONTENTS

PREFACE

Toward the end of our 1996 church Finance Convention, something very special happened to me. I began to experience what my wife, Taffi, called "holy frustration."

By every usual standard of measure, everything was going just right. The Word coming from the pulpit was good, revelation knowledge was flowing freely, and people were being delivered and set free during every service. But for a couple of nights, I went home and could neither rest nor sleep. When I told my wife about it, she said it sounded as if something was about to be born from within me. She reminded me that the last time I had such an experience, World Changers Ministries was transformed from vision to reality.

As I began to pray, study, and seek the Lord, one of the questions I asked God was, "What if a man wanted to know exactly what he needed to do in order to prosper? What would You tell him?"

In response to my question, God birthed in my spirit a revelation of the 14 steps to prosperity contained in this book. I encourage you to make a quality decision right now to follow the steps I've shared within these pages. They are designed to change your finances, your marriage, your family, and your world for the better. This book, like all the others I've written, is based on the Word of God. I am nothing apart from the Word, I can do nothing apart from the Word, and I can write nothing apart from the Word. To effectively read this book, keep your Bible close by. So, get your Bible, get into an attitude of receiving, and get ready to increase in the Word of God.

Introduction

Money is usually the first thing that comes to mind when the subject of prosperity is brought up. We've been conditioned by the world to believe that a person with a lot of money is prosperous, and if prosperous, then certainly happy.

No doubt about it, having the funds to go wherever you want and do and buy whatever you please is a good thing—but it's not everything. To think about money when you hear the word *prosperity* is not incorrect, just incomplete. You see, a person can have a million dollars in his bank account and still suffer from the ravaging effects of cancer throughout his body.

Having plenty of money is the world's limited idea of prosperity, not God's. What good does it do for you to have enough money to purchase the best medical care and still not be able to lay hold of the divine health promised to you by God? Jesus came to give you abundance in your home, body, workplace, and family—not just in your wallet. And while people desire to be financially well off, they sometimes reject the message of prosperity because they associate it with greed and view it as a message intended solely for the preacher's benefit.

Perhaps you've been told that money is the root of all evil. Really? That's not what the Word of God says. If you look at 1 Timothy 6:10, you'll see that it reads, "For *the love of* money is the root of all evil" (italics added). The prosperity message, if taught from a truly biblical perspective, speaks of much more than acquiring money. You see, God is concerned with every aspect of your life.

In fact, this book is more about letting go of your money than holding on to it. It's about loving your neighbor enough that you can willingly extend that with which you've been blessed toward someone else. Now, that's biblical prosperity!

It's time for us as Christians to have our minds renewed to reflect the good and perfect will of God. We should hear the conclusion of the whole matter rather than limit God to what He can do in our lives. Biblical prosperity is the ability to be in control of every circumstance and situation that occurs in your life. No matter what happens, whether financial, social, physical, marital, spiritual, or emotional, this type of prosperity enables you to maintain control in every situation. I'll even go a step farther and define *biblical prosperity as* "having God's ability to meet not only your needs, but also the needs of mankind, regardless of what those needs may be."

You can prosper financially, but you can also prosper in your spirit, soul, body, marriage, and life in general. How? Through the Word of God. Take David, for example. David was a man after God's own heart and, as such, reflects God's intent for us in His Word. Look at David's petition to the Lord concerning his ability to prosper. He said,

Direct my steps by Your word,
And let no iniquity have dominion over me.

(Ps. 119:133 NKJV)

Few people realize it, but David was praying for biblical
prosperity. He was asking the Lord to direct his steps according
to the Word of God. His supplication was that no evil, sin, or
wickedness be allowed to have authority over him. And if you're
familiar with the account of his life as told in 1 and 2 Samuel,
you know it took more than money to deliver him from the
many challenges he faced. David was praying for control over
everything he had to deal with, from uncircumcised Philistines
to his unforgiving father-in-law. Glory to God!

The iniquity facing David in his day may be different from
what you're going through, but the end result is the same: lack of
control. Anything in your life that controls you instead of your
controlling it should be considered iniquity. The Word of God
calls for you to be the head and not the tail (Deut. 28:13), and
more than a conqueror (Rom. 8:37).

The good news, child of God, is that an anointing is available
to put you in control of all your circumstances. You are an heir
to the Lord's promises, and David's prayer for dominion over his
life has been granted to you through the Word of God. He has
sent His Word to put back into your hands the things that have
been wrestled from you. No longer do poverty, sickness, addiction, and fear have free course to rule and reign in your life. You
no longer have to allow the circumstances of marital discord,
rebellious children, or unemployment to dominate your household.

If there are any areas of your life where you need to get back in the driver's seat, read and follow the precepts I lay out here in *Total Life Prosperity*. Meditate on the 14 practical steps to prospering in God, and get on the road to health, prosperity, and peace of mind. God has truly given you the opportunity to lay hold of the abundant life. Jesus died so that you might live.

David got the revelation that God's Word would lead him where he needed to go. He said in Psalm 119:105, "Thy word is a lamp unto my feet, and a light unto my path." If you're uncertain of how to live a prosperous life, let the Word of God within the pages of this book show you the way.

CHAPTER 1

PEACE, BE STILL

The same day, when the even was come, he saith unto them, Let us pass over unto the other side. And when they had sent away the multitude, they took him even as he was in the ship. And there were also with him other little ships. And there arose a great storm of wind, and the waves beat into the ship, so that it was now full. And he was in the hinder part of the ship, asleep on a pillow: and they awake him, and say unto him, Master, carest thou not that we perish? And he arose, and rebuked the wind, and said unto the sea, Peace, be still. And the wind ceased, and there was a great calm. And he said unto them, Why are ye so fearful? how is it that ye have no faith? And they feared exceedingly, and said one to another, What manner of man is this, that even the wind and the sea obey him?

(MARK 4:35–41)

This is one of the most well-known passages in the Bible, but I want you to see that it is also a perfect example of prosperity and the ability of God to meet the needs of mankind. Perhaps you'll get a better picture after I explain further.

Jesus and His disciples were on a ship one afternoon, right in the middle of a terrible storm. His disciples were filled with fear because they thought they were about to die. Meanwhile, Jesus was in the back of the ship, asleep on a wet pillow. We know it was wet because the Bible says the ship was filled with water. And since He was asleep in the back of the ship, and water filled the ship, we're safe in assuming that the pillow was soaking wet. (You know, Jesus must have been a hard sleeper.) Anyway, they started fussing about who was going to wake Him up, probably saying things such as:

"Luke, why don't you wake Him up?"

"I'm not waking Him up. Let Peter wake Him up."

Then John said, "Look at those waves. We're gonna die. Somebody better wake Him up!"

Matthew, clearing his throat, woke Jesus up. "Excuse us, sir, but don't you care whether or not we drown out here?"

All of a sudden, Jesus got up in the midst of the storm and said, "Peace, be still," and the wind and the sea quieted down.

Is it clear to you what happened? It was more than a matter of Jesus telling the wind and the sea to be quiet. True prosperity came over that boat. The ability of God on Jesus calmed the storm, and their lives were preserved because Jesus, in the middle of that situation, was still in control. That's the kind of prosperity the Word of God provides you—total-life prosperity.

Getting in God's presence, renewing your mind with the biblical definition of prosperity, and being obedient to the Word of God are just a few of the steps necessary to establish true prosperity in your life.

Have you ever asked someone how he was doing and he

prefaced the reply with, "Well, under the circumstances . . ."? Child of God, do you realize that you're not supposed to be under your circumstances? Through the Word of God, you have the ability to be in control of every circumstance, situation, problem, and trial you will ever face. Not only does He want you to have the finances necessary to pay every bill; He wants you to have wisdom, knowledge, patience, joy, faith, humility, and long-suffering to handle anything that might come your way. The storms and raging sea experiences in your life are subject to the burden-removing, yoke-destroying power of the anointing. Follow the rules in your Instruction Manual (otherwise known as your Bible), and those circumstances will have to obey the voice of God as it comes through you.

When evil thoughts try to attack your mind, God has given you His Word to renew those thoughts and take control over whatever is threatening your mental state. When sickness and disease try to attack your body, the Bible becomes a medicine chest, filled with godly scriptural remedies and divine prescriptions to enable you to regain control over your physical body. "It will be healing to your body, and refreshment to your bones" (Prov. 3:8 NASB).

When the enemy comes into your life and tries to cause separation and divorce, God has given you His Word to benefit your marriage. If you will make what He says your final authority on the subject of marriage, you can have control over this part of your life as well. You need not walk around in the fear that is so prevalent in the world—fear that someone will seduce and steal your mate. Draw on the wealth of the Word. Meditate on the verse that says, "Wherefore they are no more twain, but one flesh. What therefore God hath joined together, let not man put asunder" (Matt. 19:6).

I don't want you to get the idea that God is not interested in your financial prosperity because He is. As I mentioned earlier, He wants you in control of every area of your life. He wants you to be prosperous to the point that you can handle every financial situation confronting you. He wants you to be prosperous to the point that the addiction you once had can't come back to control you. This type of prosperity says that now you gain control over that addiction. It doesn't tell *you* what to do; you tell *it* what to do.

There is an anointing to put you in control of any situation in your life that is presently out of control: "The Spirit of the Lord is upon me, because he hath anointed me to preach the gospel to the poor; he hath sent me to heal the brokenhearted, to preach deliverance to the captives, and recovering of sight to the blind, to set at liberty them that are bruised, to preach the acceptable year of the Lord" (Luke 4:18–19).

As you can see, Jesus showed up in the fourth chapter of Luke and said, "I'm anointed to preach the gospel to the poor." He said, "I've got the anointing for the poor man, so he doesn't have to be poor any longer." This doesn't mean there will come a time when we will no longer have poor people, for Jesus said the poor will be with us always. It means that Jesus takes the poor man who has no control over his life and puts him back in control of his circumstances when he receives this message.

The same principle applies to the captive man and the man who is blind. Jesus was really saying that He is anointed to cause you to prosper, no matter what the situation. Whatever you lost or relinquished control of, Jesus is anointed to help you fix that situation. He is anointed so that you can get back in control.

Are there any areas of your life where you need to regain

control? You might think your life is a wreck. Maybe your husband left you. Perhaps your wife decided to call it quits, or your children act as if they've lost their minds. Before you make an ungodly decision to throw in the towel, let me tell you something. There is an anointing to put you back in control, despite what the world tells you to the contrary. The world may be out of control, but that doesn't mean you and I have to be. No, not as long as we have Jesus on our side.

You have an anointing to prosper made available to you through the Word of God, including but definitely not limited to financial prosperity. I want you to get the full picture: don't read the word *prosperity* and think only of finances. I want you to see that word and think about your entire life and all it entails because in every area and in every instance, you've been called to prosper.

As with following any road designed to take you somewhere, you have to take the first step. An old saying tells us that even a journey of a thousand miles must begin with that first step. So, what do you suppose is the first thing you have to do to begin this life of prosperity and end up in complete control of your life? How do you get to the place where you have such an ability to meet the needs of others that when a financial situation comes up, you have the money to meet that need? When an emotional situation comes up, how have you been blessed with wisdom and understanding to meet that need as well? And when temptation comes to remind you of what you used to do, what do you need in order to tell temptation to go back where it came from?

Regardless of what you've heard in the past, being able to make it through these situations is the sign of true wealth. You're walking in true biblical prosperity when you are able to handle your circumstances and not have them handle you. An even greater accomplishment than having money in the bank is not having to frantically react and respond to whatever is going on around you, but initiating your actions to line up with the Word of God. It is more desirable to be proactive rather than reactive. You come out on top of matters with the peace of God that passes all understanding (Phil. 4:7). But the prerequisite for this peace is walking with God, as you'll learn in the next chapter.

CHAPTER 2

STEP 1:
ENSURE THAT THE
LORD IS WITH YOU

~~~

The first step toward biblical prosperity is to ensure and recognize that the Lord is with you.

"But, Brother Dollar," you may be saying, "that's not necessarily true because wicked people *do* prosper. How can you say that in order for me to prosper, the Lord must be with me? I know people with a lot of money who are not living their lives for God."

If those are your thoughts, you've forgotten the definition of biblical prosperity I gave in the Introduction. Prosperity is not limited to the person who has money. The term *prosperity* cannot accurately be applied to someone who has finances to buy his children anything they want, yet lives in a house where his family members neither love nor respect one another. That's not prosperous living in the eyes of God.

If a man with God is blessed enough financially that he can be a blessing to others, he has a fantastic marriage with happy children, and everyone in the family is healthy, then he is prosperous.

Furthermore, this man will live in prosperity, even if you take away his money, mansion, and material possessions.

You simply can't stop a prosperous man. Why? Because God is with him. However, the Bible warns us that the wicked will have a form of prosperity in this world: "Behold, these are the ungodly, who prosper in the world; they increase in riches" (Ps. 73:12). Yes, it's true. Ungodly people will prosper in the world. Notice however that the verse says *world* and not that they will prosper in the *earth*.

"Well, what's the difference, Brother Dollar?"

The difference is this: the word *world* in the verse refers to the world's system—the way the world has of doing things. And that way is ungodly. It only stands to reason that ungodly people will prosper in an ungodly system. They will prosper and increase in the world's way of doing things.

That might not sound too bad to some people, but they need to know something. All that glitters is definitely not gold. Look at Proverbs 1, and you'll see that this temporal, wicked wealth is not what God has in mind for His children:

> Then shall they call upon me, but I will not answer; they shall seek me early, but they shall not find me: for that they hated knowledge, and did not choose the fear of the LORD: they would none of my counsel: they despised all my reproof. Therefore shall they eat of the fruit of their own way, and be filled with their own devices. For the turning away of the simple shall slay them, *and the prosperity of fools shall destroy them.* (vv. 28–32, italics added)

He is talking about the wicked here, the same wicked folks who were prospering in the way of the world. The Bible clearly tells us that the prosperity of fools shall ruin them!

In case you're wondering what qualifies someone to be a fool, Psalm 53:1 tells us exactly: "The fool hath said in his heart, There is no God." You know him. He believes science over Scripture, and palms rather than Psalms. He makes up the rules of his life as he goes along, refusing to pay attention to what "thus saith the Lord." The fool totally disregards God's way in favor of his own way. Look up *fool* and *foolish* in your concordance if you want to see what else the Bible has to say about this type of person. It's not pretty.

How can the same substance (prosperity) ruin the fool, yet edify the child of God? It's simple. I'll give you an example that illustrates this principle in action.

Say you know someone who is hooked on crack cocaine. What do you think he'll do with his money? Bless a single-parent family with groceries? Pay the light bill for the older couple down the street? Help his job-seeking neighbor by having résumés printed up for him? Chances are, he will do none of the above. Most certainly, he will finance his crack habit instead.

The nightly newscasts are filled with stories about rich men, famous men, who are being destroyed by their money.

The guy who is into pornography, what will he do? Spend money on his habit, no doubt, and before you know it, his habit and activities will expose him to some disease that will kill him. His prosperity will have destroyed him. You've read about this in magazines and seen it on the news time and time again—stories about people being ruined by prosperity because they were not hooked up to the Word of God concerning their lives and their wealth.

If the wicked didn't have the money, they would not be able to support those expensive habits that control them and will ultimately ruin them.

The ungodly man may possess wealth, but it cannot and will not stay with him for a lifetime. He'll end up losing it, either in this generation or in the next. God has already said in His Word that this is the outcome for this type of person.

Where does the Bible say that? Before I tell you, let me ask you a question. Did you know that every rich unbeliever on earth is actually working for you, me, and every other Christian? You may not know all your employees by name, but they work for you just the same. You probably didn't even know that you had employees, but while you have your Bible handy, take a look at Proverbs 13:22: "The wealth of the sinner is laid up for the just."

The sinners are making the money, and it's being stored up for me and you. In a sense, every ungodly rich man has a call of God on his life. He has been called to gather up riches for the last days, and according to the Bible, he will gather them up, but he won't put them on. No, that honor has been reserved for those of us who can be counted among the just. The fifth chapter of James has something to say about this important issue: "Go to now, ye rich men, weep and howl for your miseries that shall come upon you" (James 5:1).

What could possibly be misery for a rich man? The loss of his money, of course: "Your riches are corrupted, and your garments are motheaten. Your gold and silver is cankered; and the rust of them shall be a witness against you, and shall eat your flesh as it were fire. Ye have heaped treasure together for the last days" (James 5:2–3).

The man who does not serve, trust, or obey God will be destroyed by his finances because no one can operate in true prosperity without God. The initial step toward prosperity in your life is to realize that you will never have it without God. To experience true and lasting prosperity, you must be with God and God must be with you.

Do you remember reading the story of Joseph and how he was sold into slavery by his own brothers (Gen. 37:28)? Nevertheless, he was a prosperous man because he relied on God. He couldn't be stopped. It didn't matter where he was, or whether he was there by choice, chance, or force; he ended up being in control. No matter what the situation, he always ended up running things.

Joseph was forced to be a servant in the house of Potiphar, an officer of Pharaoh, captain of the guard, an Egyptian (Gen. 39:1–3). No problem. He ended up having full control of the household, running things, and keeping the entire house in order. When he was thrown into jail after being falsely accused of assaulting his employer's wife, he ended up running the jail (Gen. 39:7–23).

No matter what the circumstances may be, you can't stop a person who is prosperous in God. Material possessions do not make someone wealthy. Prosperity is knowledge of the things of God. It's the result of walking with and abiding in the King of kings and the Lord of lords. Your prosperity is made manifest when you live a life pleasing to God. Wealth that comes from above cannot be taken away.

You should know about an important aspect of prosperity. When you're prosperous in God, you don't have to look for wealth. Wealth looks for you. Sometimes, though, prosperity can't find you because it's too dark around you. Perhaps prosperity can't find you because of all the sin in your life.

I don't know about you, but I don't ever want prosperity to have trouble locating me. I want to keep my light on. I'm like that motel chain—you know the one I'm talking about. They promise to keep the light on so that you can find them. I'll continue to walk in the light of God's Word so that my prosperity can find me easily. I'll continue to live my life in the absence of darkness, in the absence of sin, because I know the wealth of God is hunting for me day and night. I won't do anything that displeases God, hinders my blessings, and prevents the goodness coming my way from reaching its destination.

No matter what happened last week, my prosperity is looking for me. And no matter what you've done, as long as you have sincerely repented, your prosperity is looking for you too.

As long as you're with God, and He is with you, your prosperity is hunting you down. Just keep the light on. Keep the sin out of your mouth and out of your life. Don't pretend that no sin is there. Just get rid of it and don't pick it up again. God can't abide in the presence of sin, and if He is not with you, neither will His ability be with you to put you in total control of your surroundings.

"And the LORD was with Joseph, and he was a prosperous man" (Gen. 39:2). Before we get into this verse, let's study the English language for a minute. Twice in the verse we find *and*, which is a conjunctive word. Conjunctions are used to hook up phrases and clauses. Whatever is on one side of the word *and* is in relationship with whatever is on the other side.

Because the Lord was with Joseph, he was walking in prosperity. Yet he didn't have any material possessions. He was considered financially poor. The fact that God was with him accounted for his wealth of life and mastery of his circumstances.

Now, it's reasonable for us to assume that if the Lord had not been with Joseph, he would not have been a prosperous man. Remember in high school algebra class, the hypothesis that if A=B and B=C, then logically, A=C? Well, the same premise applies here.

If the Lord being with you equals prosperity, and prosperity equals being in full control of your life, then the Lord being with you equals full control—that is, God being in full control. Conversely, if you're not in full control of your life, then the Lord is not with you. And if the Lord is not with you, we know that you're not a prosperous man, certainly not in the biblical sense.

It doesn't matter what you call yourself—Baptist, Protestant, Catholic, or Methodist. Make sure that the Lord is with you. I can imagine someone saying, "Well, I was born a Protestant, I've lived my entire life as a Protestant, and I'll die as a Protestant." There's nothing wrong with being a Protestant, but if the Lord is not with you, you're going to die a Protestant in hell.

At this point you may be checking the table of contents for another chapter to read, but the simple truth is, if you're without God, you're with the evil one, and we all know where he is going to end up (Rev. 20).

You see, what you do in the secret place of prayer (as well as tithing, loving your neighbor, and exhibiting other godly behavior) determines whether or not you'll be successful in this life.

Even if the doctor gives you a negative report, telling you that you will die in six months, don't despair. That doctor's report doesn't control you. If God is with you, you'll prosper even in that situation. Your attitude will control the effects of that report on you, and it will change because you abide in Christ and He abides in you.

You cannot stop a man who knows that God is with him. I don't care what environment, neighborhood, city, or circumstance he finds himself in. He has no other alternative but to succeed in God.

"And the LORD was with Joseph, and he was a prosperous man; and he was in the house of his master the Egyptian. And his master saw that the LORD was with him" (Gen. 39:2–3). Earlier I mentioned that this man had no material wealth. It was not as if his master saw the limited edition two-hump camel parked in front of the house. He was, don't forget, a servant to the rich Egyptian. The things he possessed were minimal at best.

How did Joseph's master know that God was with him? It wasn't as if God walked down the street, arm in arm with Joseph, so that everyone could see the relationship. Just what did the master see that would indicate to him that God was with Joseph? He saw that Joseph was in control of everything his hands touched and every situation in which he found himself.

Joseph's brothers sold him into slavery. He increased in knowledge, was sold to the Egyptian, and eventually was put into prison. Regardless of where he ended up, he always ended up in charge.

Don't you want that to be true of you? Once you've walked in this for a while, people will look at you and be amazed that no matter what happens in your life, you still come out the head and not the tail, above and not beneath, blessed on your way in and blessed on your way out. They can't figure it out because they thought that by now you would have given up, caved in, and quit. No one told them that when you are in Christ, quitting is not an option.

When your car broke down, no one knew because you still showed up on time, even without your car. You were laid off, and the bills still got paid. Your husband left you, and you were still able to draw on the wisdom of God to keep your household together. How? Because the Lord was with you.

People will notice that and realize there is something about you they don't understand and don't want to mess with. That's exactly what Joseph's master saw. He knew that there was some type of divine protection or influence on everything Joseph did.

Joseph was a servant. You may be a maid or a mechanic, an astronaut or an accountant. It doesn't matter what job you hold. Just make sure that while you're on the job, the Lord is there with you. That way you'll prosper. An anointing is available to draw prosperity to you. Joseph was going about his business, walking with the Lord, and the anointing available for prosperity continued to be drawn to him. This force is powerful if you will allow it to operate in your life.

As soon as Jesus arrived, that anointing to prosper acted like a magnet, drawing wise men with gifts of gold, frankincense, and myrrh. Those were not cheap gifts, either. Prosperity attached itself to baby Jesus immediately, and that same gift to prosper has been given to us as heirs of Christ.

Moses was another one who had an anointing to prosper. He was on top of the situation even when he came up against the Red Sea and it looked as if there were no place to go.

He is a perfect example of how a man with this anointing—a man who knows God is with him—will behave. He can come to a place in his life where it looks as if there is no way out—no way to get to the other side—and he will cross with dry feet. He can get to the point that it looks as if he is going to drown and still manage to keep his head far above the water.

The man who walks with the Lord will stand still and watch for the salvation of the Lord. He will know in his heart that the Lord is with him and that everything is going to be all right. And he will respond accordingly.

Perhaps you've had a comparable "Red Sea" experience in your life. Perhaps you were in a place in your life where it seemed as if you were stuck and couldn't get past that particular spot. Then all of a sudden, you realized that the Lord was there with you. That revelation opened up your Red Sea, whatever it may have been, and dried out the muddy ground. You remembered you were walking with the Lord. When you got to the other side of your dilemma, the side where you had it all under control, you knew then you were walking in prosperity.

When someone looks at you in amazement and wonders how you were able to get over, tell him that the Lord brought you through. He'll probably patronize you and say, "Yes, I know all about the Lord, but let's be real. Tell me how you really got through all that mess and came out of it in one piece." Pray for him, and tell him that, without the Lord, you could have done nothing to push that sea out of your way.

That truth reminds me of a time when someone came up to me and started behaving in what I can only term a *religious* way. I don't know what comes over some people when they're talking to a minister, but they tend to get a funny look on their faces and their voices get deep and have a theological tone. Such people usually refer to me as "Reverend."

Perhaps it is just because of my past experience in traditional churches, but whenever someone calls me Reverend Dollar, I can't help feeling as though I'm about to be conned. I prefer to be addressed as Pastor Dollar because that's what I've been called to do—pastor. Anyway, he said, "Reverend, I'd like to know . . . where did you receive your education to pastorrrrr the World Changers Church International?"

I was laughing on the inside and thinking, *Mister, you know you don't usually talk like that.*

16

When I told him that I personally did not know how to pastor, he laughed. "Well, then, how are you doing what you do?" he wanted to know.

I told him that the Lord was with me and that when something comes up that I don't know how to do, I ask Him, and He shows me how.

He laughed again. "That's a very ah . . . theoretical point of view."

"No," I said, "it's not a point of view. It's how I do what I've been called to do." After all, he did ask me how I was able to pastor my church. And I told him exactly how.

I never attended a school of theology. I've always gone to the place of "kneeology." That's where I got my degree. That's where I go to keep my credentials to lead so great a number of people, even to this day.

I call it the College of Kneeology, and God is the dean. I stay on my knees until I hear from God. Once I hear from God, I can get up from my place of prayer and do what He has instructed me to do. I'm a lifelong student, and I don't intend to graduate until Jesus comes back. He says in His Word that we are the sheep of His pasture. Well, I'm one of His sheep, and I'll get my sheepskin (otherwise known as a degree) when Jesus returns.

The Bible warns us not to be deceived. Without Him, you can do nothing. Without Him you cannot have total biblical prosperity. Don't be deceived into thinking otherwise. Men don't meet your needs. Money doesn't even meet all your needs. It can buy medical care but not divine health. Only God can give that to you.

Since men don't meet your needs, it's a waste of time to try to manipulate people into meeting your needs.

I don't write letters to my ministry partners to get anything. I write to them to *give* something. This ministry is not on television because we're trying to get something. On the contrary, we're trying to give.

I've been advised by some who look at the ministry's bottom line to go off the air in certain areas because of the cost. My response was: first of all, we don't broadcast to the lost because we're looking to get anything out of it. What could possibly be of greater value than saved souls? We look at the number of households that are tuned in and see how many lives we're touching with the message of the gospel. Often, we decide to stay in a market for a while regardless of whether the corresponding figures are in the black or in the red. We want those people who need to hear from us to have the opportunity to learn about the things of God. We stay put and teach listeners how to grow in Christ, how to love one another the way Christ loves the church, and how to prosper.

The cost to the ministry should not be and will never be our main concern. Not when we have a God who has promised to prosper us. Not when we can believe the Word of God that tells us to give, and it shall be given back to us in good measure and running over (Luke 6:38).

Our success is inevitable. The Bible clearly tells us what will happen when we give of our time, talent, and treasure. We will receive a harvest for our labors. But you have to know that the Lord is with you. I can't repeat that enough. When the Lord is with you, the grace or the anointing to prosper will also be with you. They go hand in hand—the presence of God and the anointing to prosper.

"And Joseph found grace in his sight" (Gen. 39:4). It's a good thing that Joseph found this grace in the sight of his employer, but it's more important for you to be where the Lord can see you.

You have to be in His sight in order to receive grace to be prosperous in whatever you do.

Remember what the Bible tells you in Deuteronomy 8:18 (NKJV), lest you forget that you need the Lord with you to prosper in the right way: "For it is He who gives you power to get wealth."

CHAPTER 3

STEP 2:
KNOW GOD'S WAYS
AND HOW HE OPERATES

⬛⬛⬛

If you want to prosper in your spirit, your soul, your body, your family, and your marriage, you must learn God's way of doing things. That is Step 2.

There are specific ways in which you can have control over all these areas of your life. Instead of waking up every morning hoping that something good will happen, you can take responsibility for those good things happening by learning God's method of operation.

I want you to understand first of all that praying, attending church, tithing, and living an upright life are not just things your pastor preaches to have something to say. They are life-and-death principles from God's infallible Word: "Ye shall walk in all the ways which the LORD your God hath commanded you, that ye may live, and that it may be well with you, and that ye may pro- long your days in the land which ye shall possess" (Deut. 5:33).

Notice that if you keep the commandments and walk in

God's ways, all will be well with you. But how can you walk in His ways if you don't know what those ways are? You certainly know that praying is a component of walking in His ways. That's true, but how can you prosper in your prayer life if you don't know how to pray? And what about treating your wife the way God would have you treat her? Some people have learned everything they know about how to treat a spouse through the poor examples they had while growing up.

If Uncle Festus beat Aunt Azalea whenever he became upset, cheated on her, and cursed at her, you need to know that's not God's way.

To prosper in your marriage, you must learn from the Creator of marriage how you are supposed to love, honor, respect, and submit to your mate. That's God's way.

Submission means to get "under the mission" of another. That's not just for wives. I mean husbands too. There are occasions and seasons in which the husband has to get under the mission of his wife. The smoothest way to conduct any household is for both partners to learn how to submit. Yes, submit. This caveman mentality of some men that makes them think they're supposed to give all the orders around the house will have to go if the marriage is to operate according to the will of God— not only operate, but thrive.

Submitting yourselves one to another in the fear of God. Wives, submit yourselves unto your own husbands, as unto the Lord. For the husband is the head of the wife, even as Christ is the head of the church: and he is the savior of the body. Therefore as the church is subject unto Christ, so let the wives be to their own husbands in every thing. Husbands, love your wives, even as Christ also loved the church, and gave himself for it; that he might sanctify and cleanse it with the washing of water by the word ... So ought men to love their wives as their own bodies. He that loveth his wife loveth himself ... For this cause shall a man leave his father and mother, and shall be joined unto his wife, and they two shall be one flesh ... Nevertheless let every one of you in particular so love his wife even as himself; and the wife see that she reverence her husband. (Eph. 5:21–26, 28, 31, 33)

Husband, how do you submit yourself? Find out the way God intends for you to live your life as a married man, and govern yourself accordingly. It's the same for a wife. You are to conduct yourself in your marriage the way God would have you behave. When both mates do as the Word instructs in this area, each is submitting to the other in the respect of the Lord. You are learning the biblical way to have complete control over the circumstances that come up in your marriage, and not the way of the world.

On the other hand, if you want to take the advice of a radio talk show host—advice that tells you to throw your spouse out the first time he makes a mistake or that you have to learn to assert yourself in every situation—then your marriage will not succeed.

After a while in most marriages, the problems are all about the same. We've gotten to the point that we can plot the stages of a typical marriage. There is a chart that lets counselors know what to expect people to go through during their first year of marriage.

Before most couples get married, everything is a Kodak moment—a slow-motion experience. Hair blowing in the wind. Running to meet each other from opposite sides of the cornfield—you get the picture. Once they've been married for a while, they want to speed things up.

Let me tell you something. God created us, and He designed the system of marriage. Just as you wouldn't have a Toyota mechanic work on a Ford engine, why would you trust an unsaved person to counsel you about your marriage? The Bible says it plainly enough: "Blessed [empowered to prosper] is the man that walketh not in the counsel of the ungodly" (Ps. 1:1). Since God is our Creator, isn't it reasonable to assume that God would understand how we are to function?

Have you ever noticed that in the glove compartment of every car there is a manual of operation? The makers of video-cassette recorders include a manual of operation in every box—and most people still don't know how to work the things! They have to ask the kids for help whenever they want to do something more complicated than turning them on.

All too often, we handle our lives the same way. We look to one another or some heathen expert for advice and example instead of picking up the Manual of Operation for human beings—the Bible.

You need to read the Bible. "But, Brother Dollar," you may say, "these days everyone has a different interpretation of the Bible." If that's your excuse, we can address that issue right here and now.

As for there being different interpretations of the Bible, you have a valid point. The way I see it, there are *two* interpretations of the Bible—the right one and the wrong one.

Don't be deceived. Don't let the fact that there are several translations and varying interpretations of the Bible lead you to believe that the Word of God is not true.

Think about it. There are several languages on earth today.

God put us on the earth and scattered us because He has a *world* vision, not a *tower* vision where everyone stays in one place. That's what the Tower of Babel was all about. Languages are in place, and there are rules for interpreting each language.

As a former English teacher, I'm aware of the rules of grammar and usage (although I don't always follow them). I'm also aware that there is a right way and a wrong way to interpret words. Now, when I see words in the Bible, I read them and I define them. But instead of using an English dictionary, I use a Greek-Hebrew concordance to discover the meaning of the words in the original language. I do so to make sure I understand what is being said.

If a word is in Hebrew, I go back to the Hebrew text of my concordance, find out what the word is, get the definition, and plug it into the sentence. The problem is that we try to read things in the Bible that are not there and take things out of context to the point that we cannot apply the teachings to our lives.

There is only one way to interpret the Bible—and that's the right way. The problem is, if a man is not born again and filled with the Holy Spirit, much of the Bible will be a mystery to him. The Bible has been written so that Spirit-filled people will be able to read it and understand. Those who are not born again will not be able to see God's way of doing what He does. So drop that excuse, and stop allowing the devil to deceive you in this area.

Some people convince themselves that the Bible is some man's interpretation; therefore, they reason, there is no point in reading it. Why read the Bible? Because the Bible is the written, inspired Word of God: "All Scripture is given by inspiration of God, and is profitable for doctrine, for reproof, for correction, for instruction in righteousness" (2 Tim. 3:16 NKJV).

Don't fall for Satan's line about the Bible being inspired only by man. Certainly, God used human vessels to get it written, but that's the way He operates. He uses those of us on earth who have allowed ourselves to be suitable for the Master's use. So, if that has been your excuse for not reading the Bible, then you've just lost it because it doesn't hold water.

All you have to do is read the Manual. If anyone knows how we are to operate, the Owner, our Creator, should know. Don't run around trying to figure out what's wrong in your life. Open the Manual, and it will tell you why you're not prospering, why you have no friends, or why you and your spouse don't get along. Even better than that, it will tell you how to get broken things fixed as any good manual is supposed to do. Here is an example:

> Let the wicked forsake his way, and the unrighteous man his thoughts: and let him return unto the LORD, and he will have mercy upon him; and to our God, for he will abundantly pardon. For my thoughts are not your thoughts, neither are your ways my ways, saith the LORD. For as the heavens are higher than the earth, so are my ways higher than your ways, and my thoughts than your thoughts. (Isa. 55:7–9)

God wants us to know His ways because they're better than ours. God has already come up with a way to do everything we're trying to do. As we read in Psalm 103:7, "He made known his ways unto Moses, his acts unto the children of Israel."

Did you notice what that said? He made His *ways* known unto His servant Moses, but the children of Israel knew only His *acts*. They knew what God had done, but they didn't understand the method by which He was able to get those miraculous things to happen.

Think about what those miracles actually were. They were

inducements for the children of Israel to want to know more about His ways. They didn't have a clue about the way God did things in the beginning because there was no advertising to spark their interest. Why should they have been motivated to know how God operates?

But once God came around and showed them a thing or two—once He gave them a glimpse of what He is capable of doing—He had their complete attention. He rained manna from heaven as a source of food. He gave them water out of a rock to quench their thirst. He had even opened up the Red Sea, permitting their escape from Pharaoh and his boys. After those demonstrations, their attitudes changed somewhat. They wanted to know more about God's way of doing what He did.

Remember when you were first born again. If you're like most people, spiritual things happened quickly for you then. You prayed a prayer, and your answer came almost immediately. You sowed a seed, and you reaped your harvest right away. But after you had been saved for a while, perhaps things didn't seem to happen as quickly as in the beginning. Why? Because it's time for you to learn God's ways.

One time, after I'd been reading this passage of Scripture, I went to God in prayer and asked Him when He showed Moses His ways. To answer, the Lord took me to Exodus 24:17–25:1 (NASB): "And to the eyes of the sons of Israel the appearance of the glory of the LORD was like a consuming fire on the mountain top. And Moses entered the midst of the cloud as he went up to the mountain; and Moses was on the mountain forty days and forty nights. Then the LORD spoke to Moses."

Remember those forty days Moses spent in the presence of God on the mountain? During those days and nights he spent with God, Moses received a word that changed his entire situation.

You see, child of God, it's in His presence that you begin to learn how He does what He does. He will show you how to get from one point to another. When you enter His presence, He will show you a way of operating that is higher than the way you've been trying.

If you're a businessman, getting in the secret place with God will enable you to excel in your business in a way you previously have not been able to achieve. True prosperity, the greatest prosperity, takes place in the presence of God. Too often, however, we go outside the presence of God and try to battle a problem on our own. We simply can't be successful without God.

You can never pray too much, and you can never spend too much time with God. When you have a life-changing idea, don't make the mistake of thinking that it came from you because it doesn't happen like that. That idea or thought came because you invested daily time with God, and now you have something to show for it. But it will cost you something. The price you pay is the time you spend in daily prayer with the Lord. It has cost me something to arrive at these 14 steps that I'm sharing with you now.

When a man is in the presence of God, he no longer has to wonder what in the world is wrong with his wife. God will show him exactly how to treat her, love her, and show her how much he cares. It can all be learned in His presence. Not in conversation with the boys during lunch. No, that is not the way.

I'm speaking from firsthand experience here. I learned how to treat my wife, Taffi, in the presence of God. I must be honest with you. When I married her, I was wondering, "What's wrong with this picture? She doesn't like what I like, and I don't like what she likes."

But in the presence of God, I found out how much changing I needed to do. In the presence of God, I saw that God wasn't dealing with me about Taffi; He was dealing with me about myself. I went to God and asked, "What's wrong with this woman You've given me?" I'll never forget what He said: "*You* are what's wrong with her."

Until I spent time with the Lord on the subject of my wife, I had no idea how selfish I had been. He showed me not only how to love my wife, but also how to extend that love to the members of my church, my partners, and my friends. He taught me how to express love for all of them through the things that I do and how to take their lives seriously in my hands and guard them through prayer. In the name of Jesus, I will continue to maintain that standard.

The presence of God will lead you into prosperity. Those of you who are praying diligently, don't stop because your reward may be five minutes away from manifestation. Don't slam the door on the things for which you're believing God. The wisdom of God is waiting to explode inside you and make the difference between an average lifestyle and a supernatural one. God wants to speak to us. Look, for example, at this verse from Isaiah: "Come ye near unto me, hear ye this" (Isa. 48:16).

How much more plainly can He say it? He is telling you to come near Him and hear what He has to say. He is saying, "My dear child, you're over there struggling. Come here and let Me tell you something. See, you're out of control over there in that situation. Come here and let Me show you how this thing is supposed to be done."

Notice, however, what He asks you to do before He can get you to prosper. He asks you to "come" to Him.

All this time you had your mind set on going to that popular Bible college, and He is telling you to come near to Him. He is saying in effect that it won't do you any good to go to that college anyway, without coming to Him first. There is nothing wrong with that college, it's a great school, but you first must come to Him.

"I have not spoken in secret from the beginning; from the time that it was, there am I: and now the Lord GOD, and his Spirit, hath sent me." Look at the rest of that verse and what follows: "Thus saith the LORD, thy Redeemer, the Holy One of Israel; I am the LORD thy God which teacheth thee to profit" (Isa. 48:16–17).

God causes you to gain advantage. He wants to give back to you the advantage you've somehow lost. He wants to show you how to profit and prosper. He doesn't like for His children to be the tail; He wants them to be the head (Deut. 28:13)!

If you come to Him and hear Him out, He has something to tell you that will give you the advantage over your circumstances: "Which leadeth thee by the way that thou shouldest go. O that thou hadst hearkened to my commandments! then had thy peace been as a river" (Isa. 48:17–18).

God knows the way you should go. If you would come to Him and hear what He has to say on the subject instead of listening to your unsaved friends (Ps. 1:1), you would have peace as a tranquil river about your situation. Yet some people still can't appreciate or accept the need to spend time with the Father. Everything you're sweating for, God already has and wants to give to you so that you can live a life filled with sweatless victories.

You don't pray to appear religious, and you certainly don't pray to announce to everyone the manner in which you spend your time. You pray for a reason. You get on your face before God because God has something to say to you that will cause you to prosper in every situation and circumstance you will come up against. One word from God can change your entire life. The answers you need are with Him and in His presence.

Being in control of your life is more than going to church on Sunday. Anybody can do that. Suppose God decides to give you the answer on Tuesday instead of Sunday? In the event your church doesn't hold a service on Tuesday, it would be to your advantage to have personal time with God every day. You didn't get saved just to go to someone's church on Sunday. You got saved to have a personal relationship with Jesus.

I teach the members of my church that it's vital for them to learn how to prosper for two reasons. First of all, God has given us the power to do so, and it grieves His Spirit when we don't walk in the prosperity He has already given us. Second, I teach them the Word on prosperity so that I won't be the only one walking in it. If I'm the only one prospering, outsiders will then feel as if they have a right to falsely state that the preacher is taking the money. But if we're all prosperous, they will have to recognize that the tithes are being brought to the High Priest, Jesus, and He has poured out a blessing on the entire congregation from the open windows of heaven.

A key to operating in that kind of prosperity is getting to know God's ways and how He operates.

STEP 3:
RENEW YOUR MIND
WITH THE WORD OF GOD
ON PROSPERITY

~~~

If you're going to walk in the level of prosperity that is available to you, you're going to have to be serious about renewing your mind. That is Step 3.

Failing to renew your mind means allowing your old ideas and old ways of thinking to continue to block what God is trying to get you to realize concerning your prosperity. When your mind has not been renewed, you tend to function with what I call a "ghetto mentality." All the while God is trying to show you something better.

He makes it clear in the first chapter of Genesis that He created man in His image and in His likeness. He created us so that we would resemble Him and learn to operate in His image and in His likeness. The world has infiltrated the minds of people, causing them to think one way, yet God is letting us know that the world has a way of deceiving folks.

God never created us to think and behave as if we were not worthy of the best that life has to offer. He wants us to think and behave like the King's kids that we are. Here we are under the table trying to find crumbs on the floor when it is God's intent for us to sit at the table and partake of the things He has prepared for us.

If you don't renew your mind to think like a child of the King, you'll never attempt to achieve greatness. You'll always be satisfied with mediocrity. You'll always settle for average. You'll be satisfied with minimum wages or with working for someone else because you heard somewhere you'd never amount to anything, and you believed it.

Prospering goes beyond sowing your seed because if you sow your seed and you still don't think you have a right to have certain things—or if you think, *Surely God won't do that for me*—you're defeating your purpose. You must line up your mind with God's will. Long before you plant the seed, your mind has to be one with God's will. The foundational Scripture for this step leading to prosperity is found in the book of Romans: "I beseech you therefore, brethren, by the mercies of God, that you present your bodies a living sacrifice, holy, acceptable to God, which is your reasonable service. And do not be conformed to this world" (12:1–2 NKJV).

That means this world's system. Do not be conformed to the way the world does what it does. Don't become the world. Don't turn into the world. The fact of the matter is, that's exactly what the church is doing. It amazes me how the churches all know and adhere to worldly styles and trends, especially when the Bible specifically tells us to do otherwise.

A lot of worldly stuff is implanted in you. If you were not brought up in a Christian home, the way you think and the things you do have been gathered from the world's system. And if you came from a traditional Christian family where the Bible was never seen as the final authority in your home, you no doubt have the same mind-set as if you had been brought up without the Word.

The good news is that you don't have to remain that way. The good news is that you can go through a transformation and be like Christ. All my life I've been taught that you're supposed to be poor or sick or both. How do you change from a state of self-esteem so low that you live each day being afraid of failure? How do you change from having a poverty-stricken mentality to having exactly what God wants you to have and to being exactly what He says you can be? The Bible tells us in Romans 12:2 (NKJV): "Be transformed by the renewing of your mind."

Transformation starts in the mind. If you are going to change from where you are presently to where God wants you to be, you will have to follow the law of transformation. That will call for the renewing of your mind. You will not be able to change until you first affect your mind. How's your thinking?

When I was growing up, I used to watch a cartoon series called the *Transformers*. It was about a group of Autobots—cars that could change into giant robots. They were the good guys and fought against Megatron and the Decepticons, who were able to change into aircraft. The leader of the Autobots was a big eighteen-wheeler that could transform into a huge robot named Optimus Prime. The key to his success dwelled in his heart, or matrix.

You had to watch out for the Decepticons because it was their job to deceive the Autobots. They would make them think one thing when in actuality they were doing something entirely different. The Autobots had to come out of the car mode and transform in order to fight the Decepticons.

Well, let me bring my point home. These days, we're surrounded by human decepticons from the world. They will try to tell you that you're poor, you're sickly, and you'll never amount to anything. These deceived folks will try to make you think that you're not supposed to be any better off than you are right now. But, child of God, I'm telling you that it's time for you to transform, and it has to start with the renewing of your mind. The Word needs to become part of your way of thinking.

Listen to Christian tapes and music. Watch Christian videos. To be successful at this, you'll have to get in the presence of the Word. Read, study, and meditate upon it. Read books that supplement the Word. Don't waste your time reading trashy novels or fiction books that have no bearing on your salvation or prosperity.

Don't let anything go through your ears but the Word of God until what you used to think has been changed by what is being put into your mind from the Word. That's how you renew your mind. You can't just renew those old thoughts and ideas by saying, "Ooooh, Holy Spirit." You must do practical things. Put in a tape, open up the Bible, read it, do it, act on it, and listen to music that lines up with the Word. Whatever you do, stop listening to that music with lyrics about climbing up the rough side of the mountain.

We read in Mark 11:23: "Verily I say unto you, That whosoever shall say unto this mountain, Be thou removed, and be thou cast into the sea; and shall not doubt in his heart, but shall believe that those things which he saith shall come to pass; he shall have whatsoever he saith."

As you can see by this verse, God has not called us to be mountain climbers; He has called us to be mountain movers. Faith moves mountains. When you put yourself in a position to hear the Word, hang around the Word, and expose yourself to the Word constantly, you will create patterns or strongholds in your mind. The method you used to get all that worldly stuff inside you and let it become a part of your thinking and your life is the same method you use to get the Word to become a part of your life. You should expose yourself to the Word in any way, shape, or form possible. These are what I call practical methods of transformation.

Renewing your mind and your thought life is a vital step in this process of prosperity. I have discovered (and the Word will back me up) that it is not the big things in life that stop people from becoming successful, but it's the small things, "the little foxes, that spoil the vines" (Song 2:15). The little, seemingly insignificant things end up being the reason for a person not becoming as successful as the Word of God says he can be.

Take a look at 3 John 2, which states: "Beloved, I wish above all things that thou mayest prosper and be in health, even as thy soul prospereth." This Scripture begins with the word *beloved*. Who was the writer referring to? The sinner, the unsaved person, the person who says in his heart that there is no God? Ephesians 1:6 declares that God has adopted us unto Himself and has made us the beloved. The writer was talking about those of us who are children of the King.

I'm glad the writer put the reference to health in the verse in 3 John so that you could have further evidence that prosperity is not limited to money. You can have health prosperity as well as wealth prosperity. If you pass over this verse too quickly, you might not get the full revelation the writer wants you to get. John was saying that the extent to which your soul prospers will determine the extent to which you prosper in general, including your health.

Man is a tripart being. He is a spirit. He doesn't have a spirit; he *is* a spirit, who possesses a soul and lives in a body. The soul of a man, as it is used here, is the mind, the will, and the emotions of that man. It's the area that houses memory and thought processes.

The Bible says you need to affect your soul man if you're going to have an impact on the remaining areas of your life. If you want to prosper in your life, you have to first affect your thought process. In other words, you need to stop being a couch potato, get into the Bible, go to church, and learn something about the Word of God.

It's mandatory that you expose your soul to the Word of God because you cannot go any farther than your thoughts and you cannot think any farther than what you know. If you're not learning new things daily and finding out what the Bible says, you have arrested your development. You will keep doing the same things and expecting different results, which is the definition of insanity.

Nothing different will happen in your life if you are continuing to do the same things and are not renewing your mind to the reality of the Word. Something has to change, and that change has to begin with you in the area of your mind. It's crazy for you to expect God to do anything different for you when you have not done anything different for Him.

How can you expect a million-dollar harvest when you don't tithe and you keep planting the same $2.50 as an offering? If you want to prosper in your finances, you had better give your soul more information about financial prosperity. Likewise, if you need to prosper where your body is concerned, educate yourself on the ways in which to have control over your physical self.

A friend of mine in Oklahoma has conquered the cancer

that invaded his body. When I saw him, I told him that he looked as if he was prospering in his health. He responded with a "thank you" but went on to say that he had asked God how he opened the door for cancer to come into his body. He asked the Lord where he had been ignorant in this area. The Lord told him that his ignorance was due to a lack of information on how to eat properly and how to take care of his physical body.

All that time, my friend thought he had done something spiritually wrong to bring about the disease. What God dropped in his spirit is worth repeating because you may be in the same position. God told him that lack of knowledge in any area of his life, spiritual or physical, would destroy him. "My people are destroyed for lack of knowledge" (Hos. 4:6).

It's not just an absence of Word knowledge that will get you; you need to be informed about natural things since you live in a natural body. You need to be informed about the proper care of your body in addition to knowing what to do to impact the spiritual realm. God can heal your body, but with a lack of knowledge you can turn around and die the next day because you didn't have information about healthy living.

Ignorance never has been, nor will it ever be, blissful. I don't care what that old saying tells you. What you don't know can and will hurt you in your wallet, your body, your marriage, and your life in general. But as I said earlier, you must have soul prosperity in order to prosper in general.

Are you willing to change your way of thinking? If you've been conditioned to think that God wants you to be unsuccessful, you need to think again. That's not what the Word says. Stop depending on preachers who seldom open the Book to tell you what's in it. Don't even take my word for it. I challenge you to read the Book and find out for yourself.

Stop being what I call a "welfare Christian"—you are content to accept whatever someone is willing to give you about the Word without making the effort to get it for yourself. Get down on the floor on your face in the presence of God until He speaks to you and confirms the things you read in the Bible.

Proverbs 23:7 states, "For as he thinketh in his heart, so is he: Eat and drink, saith he to thee; but his heart is not with thee." It's hard to do something when your heart isn't in it. Try to do something such as sowing seed without having your heart fully in it. The Bible talks about a man whose heart is in his giving: "As a man thinketh, so is he." Whatever you think about yourself, that's who you are.

If you think you're supposed to be poor, I wouldn't be surprised if that's exactly what you are. If you think you're supposed to depend on the government all your life for support, I wouldn't be surprised if that's where you are presently. If you've let your race or background bring you to a place of thinking negatively about yourself, that negative thinking will affect the rest of your life.

Let me give you an example of ending up where your thinking takes you. Do you know how a recession starts? Someone has to declare a recession. Then people become fearful, and they stop spending. What did not actually exist in the beginning now has become a reality.

A Christian should not participate in recessions, especially when you have the opportunity to prosper based on the financial seeds you sow. The Word says, "God shall supply all your need according to his riches in glory by Christ Jesus" (Phil. 4:19).

What are you thinking about yourself right now? If you think you can have that promotion but never own the company, you won't. If you think God can partially heal you but you will never experience total healing, you won't. That's how my thinking used to be limited. I had my mind made up that I could go no farther than the world told me I could go.

The exception, however, was one hope that the world gave me: I could excel athletically. So, my quest in life was to play professional football and make the money I needed to be able to afford the things I dreamed about. But when something like that fails—either you never make it to professional status or you get there and are injured and cut from the team—then what? You will start to think of yourself as a failure because your thinking has been molded by the world and not by the Word.

When I was playing football, the coach had us memorize a poem that tapped into a truth I couldn't really appreciate until I was born again. I don't know who the author is, but the poem did its part in helping me to get out of the negative way of thinking I had adopted. Before every game, we would say this:

> *If you think you're beaten, you are.*
> *If you think you dare not, you won't.*
> *If you'd like to win but don't think you can,*
> *It's almost a cinch you won't.*
> *If you think you'll lose, you've lost.*
> *For out in the world you will find,*
> *Success begins with a fellow's will,*
> *It's all in the state of mind.*
> *If you think you're outclassed, you are.*
> *You've got to think higher to rise.*
> *You've got to be sure of yourself,*
> *Before you can win a prize.*
> *Think big and your deeds will grow.*

Think small and you'll fall behind,
Think that you can and you will,
It's all in the state of mind.
Life's battles don't always go,
To the stronger or faster man,
But sooner or later, the man who wins,
Is the fellow who thinks he can.

What I got out of that was that no matter how big the guy was in front of me, I would not be overcome. I went out on that field with an advantage because I already believed that I was victorious. You need to come to that point too. You have to say to this big old world, "You may think you have me down, but I think otherwise. I'm going to change the way I think because I'm not a failure. I'm a somebody. God did not make a mistake when He created me."

Child of God, I don't care how you came into this world. Don't let your parents tell you that you're a mistake. Just because they didn't plan for your arrival doesn't mean that God didn't plan for you to be here. Even if you came out of an adulterous relationship or a rape situation, you're still not a mistake. God knows what He is doing, and He knows how to create: "Every good gift and every perfect gift is from above, and cometh down from the Father of lights" (James 1:17).

I'm telling you that God did not make any mistakes when He brought you into the fold. He did not make you a homosexual or a drug or pornography addict. He made you perfect in His sight, in His image, and in His will. He knows what He is doing. And if you are any of the above, just go back to the earlier Scripture concerning a man and how he thinks. For those of you who have been told that God made you a homosexual or an addict, it's a lie. Glory to God! The truth is available through the Word; you don't have to suffer that defeat any longer.

If you need Scripture directly relating to what I just mentioned, read Leviticus 18:22: "Thou shalt not lie with mankind, as with womankind: it is abomination"; or 1 Corinthians 3:16–17: "Know ye not that ye are the temple of God, and that the Spirit of God dwelleth in you? If any man defile the temple of God, him shall God destroy; for the temple of God is holy, which temple ye are." God also warns in 1 John 2 not to love the things of the world such as "the lust of the eyes," or wanting whatever your eyes have fallen upon.

You can't be delivered from something unless you first have knowledge that certain practices are sins in the eyes of God. Remember what I told you in the introduction: God wants us to prosper in every area of life. So, if you are living in a way that transgresses His Word, the Lord cannot be with you. Therefore, your biblical prosperity is hindered. Once you know God's ways and turn your back on your wicked ways in repentance, total prosperity is available to you.

At one time, I felt as if there were nothing I could do about the negative, ungodly thoughts that came into my head. You may not be able to control the birds that fly over your head, but you can keep them from building a nest in your hair. Just because a thought passes through your mind doesn't mean that it has to move in and start decorating.

I'll never forget the time our church held services in the cafeteria of a local school. Unlike now, when we have more than seventeen thousand members attending service in our new sanctuary, back then we had a total of fifteen people attending service that day. Half of them were there because we had gone to the closest nursing home and picked them up. I fasted and prayed and studied the sermon thoroughly. The sermon was in me, I was consumed by it, and I was very excited about ministering.

During my message, a woman stood up and shouted, "Get me outta here!" I tried to ignore her as if it didn't bother me, but I've got to tell you, I was crushed. "Get me outta here! Get me outta here. He ain't never gonna shut up. Get me outta here!"

Well, I don't think I want to tell you what I was thinking about that woman at that time. But just because it came through my mind didn't mean that I had to open my mouth and sign for the package.

I thank God for the Word. It will show you how to handle even the evil thoughts that pop into your head from time to time, for example: "Casting down imaginations, and every high thing that exalteth itself against the knowledge of God, and bringing into captivity"—that is, capturing, arresting, stopping (Whew! I like that!)—"every thought [not some] to the obedience of Christ [the Anointed One and His anointing]" (2 Cor. 10:5).

Capturing thoughts! Until I learned the Word of God, I didn't know that I could do that. The world had me convinced that I couldn't control my thoughts, that I had to deal with them. Yet the Bible tells me that I can catch every one of them and do maintenance on my thought life. Well, that means I can use the Word of God when the devil tells me that I can't do something. Instead of sitting there and letting him talk to me without saying anything, I'll open my mouth and give him the Word: "I can do all things through Christ who strengthens me" (Phil. 4:13 NKJV).

Don't let evil thoughts wander around in your mind. Catch them, arrest them, and throw them off your property. Then open your mouth with the Word to keep evil thoughts far from you. Listen, folks, you can't arrest a thought by sitting still with your mouth closed, listening while the devil talks to you. When he tries to tell you that you're a failure, open your mouth and watch the thought quickly disappear.

Let me give you an example of what I'm talking about. I want you to count from one to ten silently to yourself. Ready? Count. Now, say, "Glory hallelujah!"

What happened to your counting? It stopped because your brain had to shut up to hear what your mouth was saying. The counting stopped when you opened your mouth. You should use the same method when the devil speaks to you and negative thoughts go through your mind. Open your mouth, speak the Word of God, and those thoughts will stop. You will capture them and bring them into obedience to the Word of God.

This is an important practice, especially for young people, to adopt. Don't let the devil tell you that you're going to fail. Say something! Tell him, "I am not a failure; I'm more than a conqueror." Don't just sit there and let the devil talk to you without responding with the Word.

CHAPTER 5

STEP 4:
RELEASE WORDS OUT OF YOUR MOUTH TO ESTABLISH YOUR PROSPERITY

In the last chapter you read how you must renew your mind and thoughts with the Word of God on prosperity. Well, along with mind renewal, you must speak words out of your mouth to correspond to the godly thoughts you're now having. The Bible tells us that "out of the abundance of the heart the mouth speaketh" (Matt. 12:34).

Once you've had a change of mind in the area of prosperity, you will out of necessity have to change the way you speak about prospering—which brings us to the fourth step. You must begin to release words out of your mouth to establish your prosperity.

The book of Proverbs contains a passage that will give you a new respect for the practice of confession. I told you earlier that you have to be on guard not to belittle the small things. More often than not, the little things turn out to be the biggest areas in which you're missing it completely.

On the one hand are those who advocate confession, and on the other hand are those who can't seem to understand the relationship between what they say and what they see. Inevitably, someone will ask, "You mean to tell me that just by opening my mouth and talking about healing, I will be healed?"

No. Other things contribute to your prospering, but you can't neglect the part that requires you to say what you want to see. Before you can get to the manifestation, before you can get to the part that produces what you desire, you must say it first. Being insensitive to the step that requires you to open your mouth is the same as ignoring the little wire under your hood that ends up being responsible for your car not starting. And all the time you thought it was the big old engine causing the problem.

According to Proverbs 18:20–21, "A man's belly shall be satisfied with the fruit of his mouth; and with the increase of his lips shall he be filled. Death and life are in the power of the tongue: and they that love it shall eat the fruit thereof." There it is in black and white, child of God! It says that the words coming out of your mouth determine whether or not you will be satisfied. As you can see, you can have words of death or words of life coming out of your mouth. The choice is yours. You can either turn on the death cycle or use the words of God to turn on the life cycle.

Isn't it amazing the power contained in something as simple as the words of your mouth? "In the beginning was the Word" (John 1:1 NKJV). Since that's how God started things, it makes sense to me that perhaps that's the perfect way to begin anything you want to do—with the Word.

The fear up until now has been that faith teachers are telling folks to name it, claim it, and confess it. That's not all that we're telling people to do; it's just a part of a total system within the kingdom of God. It's a component of various other steps in

God's method of operation. Some critics have suggested that confession is a waste of time and that all one has to do is step out on the Word. Stepping out is not going to work if your heart is not in it. And your heart is not going to be in it until you start confessing and believing the things you've said.

Two things will happen when you confess the Word. First, you're going to write it on your heart, and second, you're going to start believing what you say. This area of confession may be what you consider a small fox—that is to say, not important—but it may be the reason your vines are not prospering.

Be mindful of what you are saying. As Christians, we trust our mouths to get us saved, but we won't trust them in other areas. The Bible says that to obtain your salvation, you must confess with your mouth the Lord Jesus and believe with your heart (Rom. 10:9–10). Notice that the confession is going to affect your heart. And then it says, "With the mouth confession is made unto salvation." So, your salvation is going to be based on your willingness to use your mouth and say that Jesus is Lord. Basically, confession brings salvation into being.

Are you with me on this? Because I want to take this a step farther. If confession can bring salvation into being, it can also bring prosperity into being. The Greek word for *salvation* is *soteria,* which means "healing, safety, deliverance, preservation, the ministering of angels, and soundness."

Do you know what the writer was saying? That with your mouth you bring into being your healing, that with your mouth you bring safety and soundness to yourself. Keep watch on what you let out of your mouth because this seemingly small fox can shut down the entire system.

There is a direct connection between your mouth and prosperity: "Let them shout for joy, and be glad, that favor my righteous cause: yea, let them say continually, Let the LORD be magnified, which hath pleasure in the prosperity of his servant. And my tongue shall speak of thy righteousness and of thy praise all the day long" (Ps. 35:27–28).

Whenever I teach on joy, I make sure that people understand what joy is and what it is not. Joy is not a state of comfort or happiness based on a person's current circumstances. Joy is the inward assurance and jubilation that come from knowing the promises written in God's Word. Joy comes from what you know. Nehemiah 8:8–10 tells us about how the scribes and the priests, after having made sense of the writings of God, declared that the joy of the Lord was the strength of the people. They were joyful in their new understanding. Their joy came from what they knew.

When the doctor gives you a diagnosis that says you're going to die, you can be joyful in knowing that by the stripes of Jesus, you are healed (1 Peter 2:24). If you'll get joy, it may cause you to giggle and grin, but only after you gain an understanding of things. The instructions on what we have been told to do with our mouths cannot be ignored. We're being told to say this continually, all the time, always.

But we haven't been saying this because of greed. Most people said it just to get money. It works for money, but it doesn't stop there. Say all the time that the Lord takes pleasure in prospering His people in their spirits, souls, bodies, marriages, and everything that affects them in this life. Say that God wants you to be in control of all circumstances, not only financial ones. He wants you to be blessed to be a blessing, until all families of the earth have been blessed.

If you're a person whose habit is to say that it's not God's will for you to be healed, then you need to break that habit. It is God's will for you to be healed. If you have been known to part your lips to say God doesn't want you to have anything, pray that God will put a bit in your mouth. God wants you to have what you need as well as the desires of your heart. He is perfecting all that concerns you, and He will withhold no good thing from His child.

Sometimes we get so deep that we "deep" ourselves out of a blessing. "Maybe the Lord doesn't want me to have this," you say. Why not? "Because I sinned." Well, you're not by yourself. But you have an Advocate with the Father, and the blood of Jesus has been made available to you. If you will turn from your wicked ways, you'll bump into goodness and mercy, and you'll find the prosperity God wants to give you.

Don't ignore this commandment from God. Say it. Don't exalt yourself above the wisdom of God and say it's not necessary to confess. He said for you to say it, and He had a reason for doing that. He is trying to get some things into your hands and into your life if you'll only open up your mouth to let the goodness of God come in.

God takes pleasure in your pleasure. He takes pleasure in your being in control of your life and circumstances. He takes much pleasure in His child being in a position to provide not only for his wants and needs, but also for others' wants and needs.

Give God the glory for your healing, your wonderful marriage, and your healthy children. Give Him the glory for having a good job. If you're not working, give Him glory for the job you will get and the provision being made while you're looking for work. I will give God the glory when I'm up and when I'm down. I will give God the glory even when I don't understand why things are happening the way they happen. I will give Him the glory anyhow. And I will continuously declare, "Let the LORD be magnified, who has pleasure in the prosperity of His servant" (Ps. 35:27 NKJV).

Now, don't try to plant a seed when your heart is not in it. There is a way to change your heart if that's the case. It does you no good to talk from a position of doubt and unbelief. When your heart is wrong, the first thing you need to do is to fix it before you can confess and expect to get anything from God. If your attitude is less than godly, eventually it will manifest itself in your less-than-godly vocabulary. Don't blame the devil for stopping your progress and hindering your prosperity when your attitude is causing you not to experience the things of God. I like to say that your attitude determines your altitude, and you won't get off the ground if it's negative. Use your mouth to agree with God and assist in the establishment of your prosperity.

For example, your mind is made up that you want to be a giver, but you have doubt in your heart. First of all, admit that. Not out loud, but recognize areas where your heart has to be changed. If your heart is not into praying because you're tired or not into Bible study because your favorite television show airs on Wednesday night, seek help through the Word for your heart condition. The devil has attacked your heart to prevent certain things from coming to pass in your life. How do you change that?

"My heart is inditing [overflowing with] a good matter: I speak of the things which I have made touching the king: my tongue is the pen of a ready writer" (Ps. 45:1). Glory to God! If my tongue is "the pen of a ready writer," every time I open my mouth, I write on the tables of my heart. Can you really write on your heart? Proverbs says you can: "Let not mercy and truth forsake thee: bind them about thy neck; write them upon the table of thine heart" (Prov. 3:3).

The only way you can do that is by opening your mouth. I read some things that I didn't believe when I first started saying them. But I kept saying them until my heart lined up with the

Word of God that I was speaking out of my mouth. I don't make confessions to prove that I'm a deep Christian. I make confessions because I'm trying to get my heart to line up with the Word of God. That way, when I begin to sow and plant and believe God for prosperity, my heart and my mouth are already lining up with what the Lord has to say on prosperity.

It's not just something to do to pass the time; it's necessary to get your heart right with the Word. If there are areas of doubt in your heart, find Scriptures pertaining to that subject, and speak them out loud.

God takes pleasure in my prosperity in every area of life. The same principles I follow in my life, I'm sharing in this book with you. I intend to prosper where my finances, marriage, and family are concerned. Because I have taught my membership well from the Word concerning prosperity, I know that before long the entire congregation will be prosperous in spirit, soul, and body. My mind is in gear now. I can see where I'm going, and I don't see failure the way I used to. Nor do I see inadequacy, insecurity, or inferiority in the same way. No! I have a new set of eyes. I've put on the eyes of the Word, and I see differently now. I understand what God is saying to me, and I will be whatever God says I can be.

When you are desperate to prosper, you'll sow whatever God tells you to sow without fear. You've run out of everything the world has advised you to do. Now you are ready to do everything God tells you to do because you are desperate to live above the natural and be all He has planned for you to be.

I'm tired of that realm known as average. I'm ready for the supernatural. What about you?

CHAPTER 6

STEP 5:
MEDITATE UPON
THE WORD

~~~

If you're reading this book, you're probably as eager to experience supernatural increase and divine prosperity as I was. Something about becoming desperate seems to move the hand of God to manifest the things in your life that you've been praying for. Actually, God is the same yesterday, today, and tomorrow. He doesn't change, but when you get tired of existing in the average realm, you will do all the changing that's necessary. You will change your giving habits, your praying habits, and your habits concerning the reading of God's Word, which brings us to this crucial Step 5.

You have read the title of this chapter and may be thinking to yourself that this is a simple and somewhat insignificant practice. Remember, it's the small foxes that spoil the vines.

Meditate upon the Word.

"But, Brother Dollar, please tell me how that's going to help my prosperity." Okay, but first, let's understand what meditation is before I tell you how it will help. To meditate is to dwell on anything in thought. It means to turn or revolve any subject in your mind. It's when you ponder, imagine, bring before the mind's eye, or conceive in thought. Get this picture: you're dwelling on something in your mind.

You can meditate in several ways. One way is to mutter or speak things quietly to yourself under your breath. Another way is to speak out loud, to muse the Word. To muse is to ponder a thought and roll it over in your mind repeatedly.

I'm sure that when most people hear the word *meditate,* the first thing that comes to mind is a practice of the New Age movement. No, this is the Bible movement. We've been doing it all along; we just haven't recognized it as such. You see, before you were born again, you had lustful thoughts that you rolled over in your mind. You meditated on those thoughts. You dreamed about those thoughts. You spoke those thoughts. And eventually, it all came to pass. Now you need to take this step called meditation and use it the way God intended it to be used. He is trying to do something where meditation is concerned. We read in the psalm:

> Blessed is the man that walketh not in the counsel of the ungodly, nor standeth in the way of sinners, nor sitteth in the seat of the scornful. But his delight is in the law of the LORD; and in his law doth he meditate day and night. And he shall be like a tree planted by the rivers of water, that bringeth forth his fruit in his season; his leaf also shall not wither; and whatsoever he doeth shall prosper. (Ps. 1:1–3)

By instructing you to meditate on His Word, God is trying to get you to a position of prosperity. He is not keeping it a secret from you; He is letting you know how to prosper on purpose. He wants you to be free from lack, poverty, and the control of your circumstances. Jesus Himself let you know that when the Lord frees you, that's true freedom. He said, "If the Son therefore shall make you free, ye shall be free indeed" (John 8:36).

What is the purpose of meditation? Meditation works in two ways. When a man meditates on the Word of God, it will affect his prosperity, and when he doesn't meditate on the Word of God, his prosperity will also be affected. One way or the other, your prosperity is going to be impacted based on how you deal with this area of meditating on God's Word. You can ignore the Word and never meditate, and you'll never see the prosperity God has designed for you to enjoy. Or you can take advantage of the godly counsel from the Word, see for yourself that it works, and witness drastic changes in your life.

Look, for example, at Joshua 1:8: "This book of the law shall not depart out of thy mouth; but thou shalt meditate therein day and night, that thou mayest observe to do according to all that is written therein: for then thou shalt make thy way prosperous, and then thou shalt have good success."

God says that you should do this day and night. I've heard of people quitting their jobs so that they could stay at home and meditate upon the Word. It's amazing to me how many people are so willing to quit their jobs for Jesus. But, folks, if a person is not successful in living by faith with a job, he will never be successful in living by faith without one.

"But the Lord told me to quit my job!"

You'd better make sure you're hearing from the right lord. You don't do things because you *think* you hear. This step of meditation will help you to understand when you should do something. When should you give a sacrificial offering? Because someone came before the church and said for you to give it? And then you give your entire life savings away and you're so scared that there's no faith in your giving. That won't benefit you.

One night during our annual weeklong Faith Convention, I told my members to go home and pray and meditate over the Word before coming back to the next service to give an offering. I think some of them might have gone home and turned on reruns of an old situation comedy instead of following the counsel I gave them. They gave their offerings, and shortly thereafter our Needs Ministry was bombarded with calls from members asking how they could get assistance to keep their utilities on. The people had given sacrificially and were then in trouble with their finances. Where was the balance?

How do I know when it's time to participate in something? How do I know when it's my time to step out in faith? When God tells me to give a car away, how do I know that I'm ready for that? Understand what I'm about to tell you. There is a way for you to be in a position to do what God has instructed you to do.

Each of us has had a problem at some time or another doing what the Word says for us to do, myself included. When I came across some Scriptures, I said to myself, "Now, that's going to be hard to do." I couldn't say, "I'm not going to do it." I couldn't even fall back on the Scripture that says it's better not to make a vow than to make one to God and break it.

To make up your mind not to do it is no way out. As Christians, we should never be looking for a way *not* to do the Word of God. Instead, we should be eager to do all that the Lord commands us. If you're having a problem obeying what you hear from God, that's a sure indication that something is wrong with your heart, and that it needs to be fixed. That something is hard to do doesn't give you a reason not to do it.

Meditation will help you in this dilemma. Its purpose is for you to see your way clear to do whatever God has instructed you to do.

One Christmas season, my wife and I invited our entire family over to the house to celebrate. The week before Christmas, I was praying and asking the Lord what He would have me do for the family that year. He said, "I want you to give all your money away."

I said, "What?"

He said, "I want you to give all your money away. Cash your checks, and give to everyone who comes into your house. I want you to bless them financially." Talk about hard to do! I still had bills to pay, and at that time in my life, I was trying to get out of debt.

At that point I had a choice. I could have told the Lord I couldn't do what He said. I could also have done in fear what He told me to do. (Did you know that sowing in fear or under pressure won't bring a good harvest? Sowing in faith brings the bountiful harvest of blessings back to the sower.)

I knew that I couldn't give under pressure, but nonetheless, I had fear all over me—to the point of shaking. I was well aware of the fact that by not doing this thing, I would be disobeying God. I had heard Him loud and clear, no doubt about it. I heard exactly what He said.

So, I looked at every verse I could find on sowing and reaping, and every verse I could find on giving. Then I put the Bible down on my bed (I'll never forget this), I got on my knees, and the first thing I said was, "Oh, Lord, help me."

I began to meditate on those Scriptures concerning giving and receiving. I began to revolve them in my mind, explode them in my thought life, and say them out loud. I began to think them over, to ponder them. I did this for hours and began to notice something. After a while the Word I was meditating on became more real than my fear of giving all my money away.

I put those Scriptures in my heart day in and day out. By the time Christmas came around, I was so filled with the Word on sowing and reaping that my fear didn't stand a chance. It was a thing of the past. I had fixed my heart and got it in line with the Word of God—just in time. When people came through the door, I greeted them with, "Here you go. Take this."

What was I doing? I was standing on the Word. I meditated on that Word and even opened up my mouth to say, "Oh, I thank You, Lord, that I am delivered from debt. I thank You that I'm out of debt, my needs are met, and I have plenty more to put in store." I could do that because my heart was fixed.

You can't do what I described without first getting your heart fixed the way I got mine fixed. That has been the problem with the body of Christ. We'll do what we see others do, without having the revelation that they had when they did what they did.

One man gives a car away, and he gets a better car. Another man gives a car away because he saw the first man do that, and now he will be riding public transportation for the next six months. The difference is that one man meditated on the Word for that instance and got his heart right, while the other did only what he saw the first man do.

The purpose of meditating is to place you in a position to do God's Word. It is effortless to do the things God tells you to do once you become consumed with the Word you've been meditating upon.

That's exactly what God was saying in Joshua 1:8. You will make your way prosperous and you will have good success when you meditate on the Word day and night. Without a doubt, your prosperity is going to be based on meditating on the Word of God. The Word will give you back the control you have lost. If you've lost control in your marriage, meditate on the Word where marriage is concerned, God will speak a word to you, and something will happen to get your control back.

Someone says, "I lost my job."

I say, "Meditate on the Word."

"Well, you know, Pastor, I have some bills to pay. You're talking about meditating on the Word, but I need money."

I know you need money. That's why I'm telling you to meditate on the Word, so you can make yourself prosperous, have good success, and regain the control you can't have when you're lacking financially. I like what God said about meditating until you can observe to do. In other words, keep meditating until you see yourself doing whatever you're believing God for.

This upcoming set of questions will require complete honesty (which is no problem for a child of God). Before you were born again, did you do things you had no business doing? Before you did those things, you *saw* yourself doing them, didn't you? You saw yourself engaging in sexual activity without a marriage license.

Well, meditating on the Word is no different. Some of you used to worry constantly about things until you made yourself sick or until the thing you worried about came to pass. Worrying is a negative form of meditation.

"Oh, Lord, where is that child? She probably had a wreck." Whether you realize it or not, that's a form of meditation. You keep rolling the thought around and can't seem to get it out of your mind. You keep worrying about it. My counsel is to get rid of the negative stuff and put the Word of God in its place. Use the same system of meditation to produce prosperity in your life.

I believe you're getting this. You're not just looking for a quick and easy answer that won't require any work on your part. You see, if you fail to take the time necessary to invest in the Word of God and get out of it the things you need, you'll never have control over your life. It's definitely going to cost you some-thing. You must be willing to pay the price.

David said, "Neither will I offer . . . unto the LORD my God of that which doth cost me nothing" (2 Sam. 24:24).

Some people are so welfare minded that they want something without having to work for it. They want something for nothing. This blessing is going to cost you something.

"Well, Brother Dollar, I don't understand. If the Lord is really the God you say He is, why doesn't He give it to me?"

The same reason that no one else is going to give it to you. Because you're not making an effort to get the things He holds for you in His hands.

"But He is God. He understands."

He understands that some of us refuse to work. He understands that once some folks get a job, they do everything they can to lose it. He also understands that the devil isn't responsible for your losing your job. In essence, because you were constantly late to work, you threw your job away. It's not wise to stay out all night. The wise thing is to get your rest so that you can get up early in the morning to pray, get ready for work, and arrive on time.

When some people finally get to work, they are caught sleeping on the job. Then they have the nerve to say that the devil made them lose the job. He didn't have anything to do with the loss. Their inconsistency, noncommitment, and failure to take responsibility cost them the job.

Could this be one of those small, neglected foxes that you have let spoil your vines? As I said earlier, this will cost you something. Imagine going to church and giving an offering for which you've prepared your mind and heart. God then tells you, "I need for you to give one thousand dollars in order for Me to do what you desire."

Don't start praying in tongues and pretend you don't hear Him speaking to you. Take the word you heard from God, and find your Scriptures. Get your heart fixed. Get ready to do what He requires of you. It's not a question of disobeying God; it's a matter of obeying Him after you've gotten your heart fixed on the matter. We read in the psalm, "Praise ye the LORD. Blessed is the man that feareth the LORD, that delighteth greatly in his commandments" (Ps. 112:1).

When a man is doing God's Word, He will empower him to prosper. He will give him godly ideas or set him up for favor from men. He will open doors that the man could never have opened by himself. By blessing him at every turn, God has put this man in a position to prosper because he delighted in His commandments.

We read in the next verse, "His seed shall be mighty upon earth: the generation of the upright shall be blessed" (Ps. 112:2). Even this man's children are going to be mighty as a result of the way he lives. Blessings will come upon all of those who walk uprightly before the Lord, keeping His precepts and doing His will.

The psalmist continued, "Wealth and riches shall be in his house: and his righteousness endureth for ever" (Ps. 112:3). The psalmist was not talking about a spiritual house. No, he was saying that prosperity will be in the house of those who are righteous. If you're not upright, those durable riches will not be in your house. You have to do what God tells you to do in order to be so blessed. You have to operate in His Word.

If you don't see wealth and riches in your house, could it be that you don't fear the Lord? Maybe you're not delighting greatly in His commandments. Or perhaps you're not upright. I ask these things only because according to the Word, if you're doing all that the Scriptures say, you're supposed to be prosperous. There might be other reasons why your life is not a reflection of the Word of God.

> Unto the upright there ariseth light in the darkness: he is gracious, and full of compassion, and righteous. A good man showeth favor, and lendeth: he will guide his affairs with discretion. Surely he shall not be moved for ever: the righteous shall be in everlasting remembrance. He shall not be afraid of evil tidings: his heart is fixed, trusting in the LORD. *His heart is established,* he shall not be afraid, until he see his desire upon his enemies. He hath dispersed, he hath given to the poor; his righteousness endureth for ever; his horn shall be exalted with honor. The wicked shall see it, and be grieved; he shall gnash with his teeth, and melt away: the desire of the wicked shall perish. (Ps. 112:4–10, italics added)

The list of what God will do for those who live a life that is pleasing to Him is endless. This passage from Psalms gives us a glimpse of all that awaits us when we trust in Him. If you're going through a rough time but living right, God says He will give you the answer right in the middle of that darkness. Once your heart is fixed on the things of God, the blessings will follow. Meditating on the Word of God is the way to get your heart fixed and the method by which the blessings will begin to flow into your household.

Don't think for one minute that this is a waste of time or that no one will see the result of your efforts. It says in verse 10 that the wicked shall see what you've been spending time meditating upon. Not only that, they will see you prospering and wish something bad would happen to you, but the Bible says not to worry. No weapon in thought, word, or deed that is formed against you shall prosper (Isa. 54:17). The desire of the folks who wonder how you do what you do will perish or come to nothing.

Paul wrote, "Meditate upon these things; give thyself wholly to them; that thy profiting may appear to all" (1 Tim. 4:15). Are you ready to prosper in every area of your life? Are you desperate to do this? You cannot be concerned about what anyone thinks at this point. You cannot walk in fear or listen to negative things being said about you. You can't try to please everyone and prosper in the things of God at the same time.

Picture this: every day at work, every time a certain coworker sees you, the Word is coming out of your mouth. When he asks how you're doing that morning, you tell him that you're blessed coming in, blessed going out, and that you're magnifying the Lord. He doesn't understand why you bring your Bible to lunch. He starts teasing you and calling you "the preacher man."

Oh, that's all right. Sit there during lunchtime and ponder the Scriptures. Even on the elevator and on your break, let those Scriptures come out of your mouth, and repeat them under your breath. And when what you've been meditating on comes to pass, that same person who criticized you by saying, "It doesn't take all that," will wonder how it all happened.

Remind him of all the times he saw you reading your Bible, heard you confessing, and watched your lips move as if you were talking to yourself. Let him know how it all happened. Let him know that by doing those things he felt were unnecessary, you made your way prosperous.

The Bible says that your profit will be seen by all. When it finally comes, those who made fun of you will not be laughing anymore. No, the Bible says they will be grieved. For those of you who think it's nonscriptural that they will look on you and be saddened by your prosperity, go back to Psalm 112:10. God wants them to see you profit. In the time of trouble, they will think back and remember the Word coming out of your mouth, being kept before your eyes, and going through your ears. They will remember what you did while riding the elevator and eating lunch and wonder if it will work for them.

That's the time to let them know that if it will work for you, it will work for them, providing they follow the same steps. It's a matter of reaping what you sow. Take the time and make the effort to do certain things, and you will see the manifestation of your labor. That all happens through meditating upon the Word of God. You meditate so that you can do. Because prosperity is based on Scripture, the steps tend to blend into one another. You'll see this more clearly in Step 6.

The psalmist urged, "Stand in awe, and sin not: commune with your own heart upon your bed, and be still. Selah" (Ps. 4:4). Pay attention to the "sin not" part of that Scripture. All of it is important, but sin in your life will greatly hinder your prosperity. When you commune with your own heart or meditate on things you have placed in your heart from the Word of God, you are better able to resist the temptation to sin.

Because some folks haven't taken the time to put the necessary things into their hearts to enable them to walk uprightly before God, they have what I call "spiritual heart attacks." They have nothing written upon the tables of their hearts to rely on in time of need.

CHAPTER 7

STEP 6:
BEGIN THE PROCESS OF
SEEDTIME AND HARVEST

S o far in our journey toward prosperity, I've shared these steps: ensuring that the Lord is with you; spending time with God and knowing His ways; renewing your mind; using the right words; and meditating upon the things of God. Up to this point we haven't discussed sowing seed in detail, but now I think we're ready to deal with this very important aspect of the journey: Step 6.

Before a farmer plants seeds, a certain process is necessary to prepare the soil for planting. He doesn't go out to the field and throw seeds in the ground. He starts as far as a year in advance to prepare the ground for the seeds.

What's been happening with the body of Christ is that we've been planting our seed, but we haven't paid attention to the necessary prerequisites for preparing the field for our seed. All of the steps taken so far (and the ones to follow) will affect the ground and the potential yield from the seed.

You will never be ready for seedtime and harvest until you fix your heart to do all that God commands you to do. When you go to God and talk about your need, God is going to talk to you about your seed. I recently spent some time with Oral Roberts. This awesome man of God had more than a little to say to me concerning the manifold wisdom of the Word.

One thing he shared with me that struck an agreeable chord in my spirit was that before he does anything, he prays in tongues and plants a seed. Of course, praying in the Holy Spirit will give you the wisdom to bring the answers when you need them. The answer to the very problem or challenge you're about to face has already been released in your spirit. The only thing you have to do now is to pray that you may interpret those things that came up while you were busy praying in tongues.

When you have seed in the ground, you're not operating the system illegally by trying to believe God for a harvest when there was no seed planted. Oh, it all makes sense. It's all starting to come together.

Before I move on, I feel compelled to mention your church attendance and responsibility. I have found that some people won't even allow for enough time to be in church for an hour and a half. If that's the case with you, you won't be very successful in meditating upon the Word when you get home.

At the risk of being repetitive, I have to say again that this success in Christianity, this God-kind of prosperity, is going to cost you something. I'm not convinced that everybody is willing to pay the price.

The book of Genesis tells us, "While the earth remaineth, seedtime and harvest, and cold and heat, and summer and winter, and day and night shall not cease" (Gen. 8:22). That's some thought. Just think, as long as the earth remains, no one will be able to stop the system God has provided for planting and reap-ing. Seedtime and harvest will never fail. If you ever get to the point that you're planting and harvesting on a consistent basis, they will never fail. This verse is not only about money; it's also about life. Life itself is based on the concept of seedtime and harvest.

Paul stated, "Be not deceived; God is not mocked: for what-soever a man soweth, that shall he also reap" (Gal. 6:7). Paul told us as plainly as he knew how, "I don't want you to be deceived, child of God, because whatever seeds you plant, those are the seeds you will harvest." Notice, he didn't just say if you sow money. He said *whatsoever* you sow—good or bad, material things, spiritual things—has been implemented in this system of seedtime and harvest, and something will spring up as a result. If you don't take the seed back, if you don't cancel the harvest, it will come up and something will grow.

So, he said, don't be deceived or surprised when you see the harvest because God is not mocked. He will not be made to look like a fool. As the old folks used to say, "Whatever you sow, that's what you're going to reap. If you sow ugly, you'll reap ugly."

This thing works. An example can be found in what I've been seeing in our ministry. Folks have been sending in a lot of watches, rings, and other jewelry. We really don't encourage the gift of that seed because the ministry can't benefit from it except to give it away. Well, we took the jewelry and started planting it into people's lives, and guess what? More jewelry keeps coming in. I said to God, "We don't want that, Lord." And He said, "Well, stop planting it."

If you want to sow into the ministry, take the watches and rings and convert them into money, give it, and we'll sow it and get money in return. But as long as we keep sowing jewelry, we're going to harvest jewelry. It works, folks. I'm telling you that it really works.

Jesus said to them, "Because of your unbelief: for verily I say unto you, If ye have faith as a grain of mustard seed, ye shall say unto this mountain, Remove hence to yonder place; and it shall remove; and nothing shall be impossible unto you" (Matt. 17:20).

Are you as excited about this verse as I am? Do you have any idea what Jesus said? I know you're probably focusing on the part that says, "Nothing shall be impossible unto you," but that's not the part that excites me. If you have faith as a seed. If you handle your faith like a seed. How do you handle a seed? You plant it. If you don't plant a seed, it can't benefit you. If I leave the seeds in a bag in the barn, I won't reap a harvest from them. But if I take my faith and treat it like a seed, nothing will be impossible to me.

We all have faith, but we haven't been treating it like a seed. We've been leaving the Book in the living room on the coffee table. Treat your faith as if it were a seed, and nothing will be impossible to you.

If you've ever been in a situation where you thought you needed more faith, then you know what I'm talking about. All my life, I've heard that someone didn't get the new car, house, or job he was believing God for because he didn't have enough faith.

The disciples were once in that position: "And the apostles said unto the Lord, Increase our faith. And the Lord said, If ye had faith as a grain of mustard seed, ye might say unto this sycamine tree, Be thou plucked up by the root, and be thou planted in the sea; and it should obey you" (Luke 17:5–6).

As you can see, the apostles thought they needed more faith, just like so many of us feel we need to increase in this area. Whenever I read that passage, I feel like saying, "Are you sick of yours?" I mean your life, lack of prosperity, marriage, job. Because if you are, Jesus has the answer. If you're sick of not getting what the Word says you can have, the time has come for you to be healed. Jesus was saying that if you have faith like a seed, you can plant it, and it will obey you.

In 1 Peter 1:23, the Word is called incorruptible seed, which means it will always produce. Treat your faith like a seed, and nothing will be impossible for you—as long as you plant it in the proper soil.

We read in the book of Proverbs, "My son, attend to my words; incline thine ear unto my sayings. Let them not depart from thine eyes; keep them in the midst of thine heart. For they are life unto those that find them, and health to all their flesh. Keep thy heart with all diligence; *for out of it are the issues of life*" (Prov. 4:20–23, italics added).

Words are seeds, and from your heart come the forces of this life. Your heart is the soil in which you plant the Word of God. Seed won't grow if it's not planted in soil. Your heart is the soil for faith seeds, and faith seeds must get into your heart before they can produce anything in your life.

You learn from the Scripture that you are to "incline thine ear unto my sayings. Let them not depart from thine eyes." That's talking about the Word. Whatever goes into your ears, is seen through your eyes, and comes out of your mouth is going to get into your heart. I call them the ear gate, the eye gate, and the mouth gate. If it's on your mouth, it's going to be put in your heart. If it's in your ears, it's going to be put in your heart, and you will have whatever is put in your heart. When you plant a seed, it will grow. You will harvest whatever is in you.

To treat your faith as a seed, you have to get it in your mouth, in your eyes, in your ears, and into the soil of your heart. That's meditation. God has already invented the system of seedtime and harvest. Whatever you plant will grow. I don't know how, but plant it and it will produce. Get the Word in your heart, and it will produce what you've read.

The problem, however, is that we've been guilty of mingling seeds. We'll put the Word in our eyes, ears, and mouths and turn around the next day and choke what we've planted by using negative, faithless words.

We also read in the book of Proverbs, "Put away from thee a froward mouth, and perverse lips put far from thee . . . Turn not to the right hand nor to the left: remove thy foot from evil" (Prov. 4:24–27). A "froward mouth" is a disobedient mouth. Don't allow your mouth to speak anything contrary to what you've planted from the Word of God. Don't let anything come from your lips that will undo the good work you've done concerning your faith. The instructions given to you in that passage show you how to farm your seed. They're telling you how to guard and watch over the good seed you planted in the good soil of your heart.

Water your seed, and keep out the weeds and insects. You're working on a harvest right now, and you want to make sure that it comes back to you a hundredfold. Once you plant in good soil, your seed will grow. Nothing shall be impossible to the man who knows how to treat his faith as a seed. That seed is your servant and should obey you once you've done the proper planting.

You'll have no problem being healed now, but you can't be irresponsible and sit back looking at soap operas in your spare time. You must do some farming. If you should go to the doctor and he says you've got cancer and you're about to die, say, "Okay, Doc, see you later." Tell him you're going home to do some farming. Before you leave, though, ask him if he has a cure for cancer.

Doctors are referred to as practicing physicians. Tell him that you know a Physician who doesn't have to practice and has never lost a patient. Tell him that you have a bag filled with seed that will grow healing throughout your body.

This seed is so special, it will even work on your unsaved spouse. Look in that bag, find household salvation seed, and harvest a saved and sanctified spouse. If you're faithful to what you've planted, it will spring up before you or your spouse knows what happened.

When the Bible says that nothing shall be impossible unto the person who has faith, that means you can take every seed or Scripture that talks about money and plant it in your heart. You can declare that you're out of debt and that the Word of God has met all your needs.

While some folks are sitting around worrying about how to get out of debt, you're planting debt-free seed. They're saying, "Lord, give me more faith so that I can get out of debt." And to that God would say that He has given all the faith He can give: "I've given you My Word in the Amplified, New American Standard, King James, New King James, and New International Versions, just to name a few. I've inspired it to be written down all these different ways so that you could get ahold of it. I've given you sixty-six books filled with faith. I can't give you any more faith now because I'm resting. Take what I've already given you, and plant it. Take it off your coffee table, dust it off, open it, read it, confess it, and plant it."

Child of God, you don't have to depend on anyone else to do this for you. In the next chapter, I'll show you how to become consistent in your planting and not become weary in well doing as you travel down the path from where you are to the level of prosperity where the Father would have you to be.

CHAPTER 8

STEP 7:
STAY CONSISTENT AND COMMITTED TO WHAT YOU'VE PLANTED

Let us not be weary in well doing: for in due season we shall reap, if we faint not.

(GAL. 6:9)

By now, you've come too far to faint, cave in, or quit. Child of God, you must be consistent and committed to what you have started. This is Step 7. You must remain true to the seeds you have planted from the Word of God. If you want to experience a prosperous life, you must resign yourself to the fact that consistency is necessary. You must get a revelation of how important it is to walk the walk of commitment.

You can't do something once and expect to operate in strong prosperity. It won't happen. You can't do something every now and then or just when you feel like doing it and expect to see results. The very thought of that goes counter to the law of breakthrough.

Most folks today are surrounded by a wall of containment—
a wall that won't let them out of the minimum wage cycle, a wall
that won't let them go any farther than where they are right now.
That's not God's plan for us. He never intended for the church to
be held by this or any other barrier. To break down that wall, He
has instituted a law of breakthrough. It is a law that will work for
anyone, regardless of who you are or the particulars of your
background.

A law is an established principle that will work for anyone at
anytime. For instance, the law of gravity is not a respecter of persons. Anyone who climbs atop a building and jumps off will be
treated by gravity in exactly the same way as anyone else. I don't
care who you are, what color you are, or what town you live in,
the law of gravity works the same for everyone.

Likewise, the law of breakthrough works for anyone who
involves himself in this principle. This law says that when he operates in something consistently, it guarantees he will have a "burst-
ing out" or a "breaking forth" into what he is believing God for.

But maybe you've always thought this. You thought that if
you selected a principle from the Word and did it once, it would
produce a breakthrough or a harvest. Do it one time. Nothing
happens. You quit. You tithe one time. Nothing happens. You
quit. You try praying for an hour one time. Nothing happens.
You quit. You go to church one time. Nothing happens. You
won't be going back.

Sound familiar? Nothing will ever happen for you as long as
you fail to operate the law properly. The law says that if you want
a breakthrough, you will have to take the principle and do it over
and over and over again until something happens.

Don't ask me when it's going to happen. All I know is that
the Bible says that it will happen in due season. Your mission—

should you choose to accept it—is to repeat the process until you see results.

This law further states that this person who follows through repeatedly on a truth will begin to see walls of containment come down. Doing it once, occasionally, or only when you're in trouble doesn't bring the desired results. When you're not consistent, you're busy doing something else, which makes you what the Bible calls a double-minded man. That man is unstable in all of his ways: "Let not that man think that he shall receive any thing of the Lord" (James 1:7).

On the one hand, you have a law of consistency that leads to the breakthrough, and on the other hand, you have a law of slothfulness that leads to nothing. The problem is not that you've been doing anything wrong. The problem is that you've not been doing the right thing long enough.

You see, praying works, but you haven't been praying long enough for your prayers to work. It's a matter of loyalty. It's a matter of being a person who is willing to change your plans to meet the plans of the One you are committed to. You need a pliable heart that enables God to come in and give you directions on how to live.

The psalmist urged, "Delight thyself also in the LORD; and he shall give thee the desires of thine heart" (Ps. 37:4). For years, we've read this verse as if the word *delight* referred to enjoying yourself or having a good time. What it means in this context is to be soft or pliable. That is, if you are flexible, loyal, workable, pliable in the hands of the Lord, and willing to change at His command, then you can become prosperous in God. You may be on the road headed in one direction, but to have a soft, pliable heart, you must be willing to let God come to you and say, "That's not what I would have you to do," and you have no problem turning around.

A loyal man is willing to change his plans to meet the plans of the One to whom he is committed. Notice the next verse: "Commit thy way unto the LORD; trust also in him; and he shall bring it to pass" (Ps. 37:5). It seems to me that there is only one thing to do. Commit thy way, commit thy way, and continue to commit thy way. Most people are afraid of commitment because it requires them to produce what they've committed to and they don't know if they will feel like carrying out the promise to the end.

God loves commitment because it puts you on the line. If you're not willing to make a commitment to God, I can't imagine your being willing to do what it takes to get what you desire.

You will never be successful if you're unwilling to commit. If you're trying to establish something where your body is concerned, whether it's losing or gaining weight, it will require commitment. You can't halfheartedly do anything and expect to achieve your objective. You know, eat diet food on Monday and pound cake on Tuesday. If you're trying to build up a strong body and work out one week, then take three weeks off, it won't work. Where there is no consistency or commitment, there is no breakthrough.

How committed are you to getting hold of the things of God? It's sad to say, but too many Christians have committed their lives to Jesus by getting saved, but they have not committed themselves to His Word. When you make the commitment to do things the Word way, you have to prepare yourself for all of the consequences that may come as a result. I went around with holes in my shoes because I made the commitment to find out if God is really the provider He says He is. I had to know beyond a shadow of a doubt that He would do for me what He says in His Word. I hated it when it rained and my socks got wet, but I had to find out for myself that the Word works. And it did. It wasn't long before God spoke to someone's heart not only to buy me some new shoes but a new suit and tie as well.

I'm telling you, child of God, there comes a time in your life when you have to know for yourself that God will do for you what He says. It's not enough to hear about being free or to listen to talk about it on tape. When you get down to it, you have to know if this thing you've heard preached, this thing you've read about and meditated on, will really work for you. To find that out, you will have to go all the way with the Lord.

Most Christians will commit to begin, but their knees become a little wobbly toward the end. You run into things you didn't expect, and the first thing you want to do is to yell for someone to bail you out. When that happens, you miss the opportunity to deposit an experience into your life. In essence, you're living with all this Word inside you, but very little experience of victory. You're committed at the beginning, but you never pass the test because you're always bailing out at the same question.

When you're in school, the teacher gives makeup exams for those who don't pass the test the first time. It's time to experience the joy of coming all the way out of a trial. You'll never know what it's like to reach the mountaintop if you're one of those folks busy climbing up the rough side of the mountain. And because you don't know what this victory is like, it's very difficult for you to tell someone about commitment, never having passed the test yourself.

So, when are you going to get the deposit brought by the experience of victory? Once you have the experience, then comes the hope for you to believe for the next victory and the next one after that (Rom. 5:1–4). The experience of victory. You believed it when you heard it. You meditated on it and followed up with prayer. I mean, you really believed this thing, but something happened right in the middle of your believing God to bring this thing to pass. You gave up, caved in, and quit. You walked in doubt, lost the commitment you started out with, and left the Word behind.

Now, you've decided to do things the world's way because "this Bible thing ain't working" as you thought it would. Do you realize, child of God, where that leaves you? The tragedy is that it leaves you still not knowing for yourself whether the Word truly works. You believe it will work, but you're not completely convinced that it will work for you.

It's like the situation of the guys who coach sports franchises. Now that they're in charge of teams, they know exactly what the players are going through because they've been there. When someone comes to the sideline complaining about getting scratched up, the coach (who is a former basketball all-star) says, "Don't worry about it. It comes with the territory. Keep doing what you're supposed to do. You'll get your breakthrough after a while."

Or what about the fellow who used to play middle linebacker and now coaches in the NFL? His linebacker comes to the sideline and says, "You know, Coach, you told me to shoot that gap, but every time I get ready to shoot it, someone hits me on my right shoulder, then on my left shoulder."

And the coach says, "Hey, I've already experienced the victory. I'm a Hall of Famer, and all of this comes with the territory. I want you to be consistent. Shoot that gap. You may get hit on the left. You may get hit on the right. That's going to happen. If you'll just stay down low and shoot that gap, everything will be all right. Get down low, and let them come whichever way they choose."

When you do as the coach instructs, you experience the victory. But when someone rushes you and you give up at the first rush as if something is terribly wrong, you'll never know what could have happened because you missed your opportunity for success.

One day in your life when you have nowhere else to turn, you will have to make that quality decision. In the world, you can't qualify for a loan, and no financial institution is going to give you the money you need. As far as it is concerned, you have too much debt and don't make enough money to handle your current debts, much less take on a new one. Maybe the loan officer is prejudiced, and in her eyes you're the wrong color, come from the wrong background, or have the wrong last name. What do you do then? I'll tell you what you do then. It's time to follow the instructions, but this time follow them all the way through. Get down low, and be ready to shoot that gap. No matter what hits you, when it's time to go, get in there and shoot that gap!

For some of you, a breakthrough is waiting on you to become committed all the way to the end. You get in the fire, someone asks how you're doing, and you tell him that you're going through. It's time to come out. It's time for you to stop climbing up those mountains. The devil knows that he can't let you experience this victory because once you do, he can't fool you anymore.

Once you reach the other side, after carrying out the instructions to the end, you won't be full of doubt and fear about whether the Word works because you'll be walking in the results.

Once you've experienced healing, pain means nothing to you anymore. Knowing that someone died in your family of a certain disease won't faze you anymore. After you get a report from your doctor, believe and receive your healing, and get to the victory side, you'll have a different story to tell. You'll tell the next person, "Oh, don't worry about the pain. Don't worry about the doctor's report because it's all part of the territory. Keep moving on through." Something else happens when you can deposit this win in your heart. Never again will anyone be able to tell you that God can't do certain things in your life.

Once you've experienced something like healing, you'll be committed to the Word on healing and everything else. When bills come in, you won't be depressed because you're committed to something. It's not enough just to say you're committed in the beginning. You must stick with this thing long enough to see what the Bible calls the expected end. That's what you expected when you started out in the first place, so you may as well go all the way with it.

When you stand on the Word, you stand on what God has said. You're not the one who said it. You're not the one who brought it up. You didn't have anything to do with it. He said it. Once you say you're going to commit yourself to His way and trust Him, the Bible says that He will bring it to pass. I'm not going to let what I can't see scare me. I've got to go to the end with what I've started.

When I commit to sow a specific amount because I'm believing God for something, come hell or high water I'm not going to change my commitment. If there is nothing in the house to eat, and you want to see this thing through, maybe this is a good time to fast. I've done that before. I can't preach the Word unless I know for myself that it works. It's not enough to say you're going to stick with this thing. No, you have to go all the way to your expected end.

When I had those old shoes with the holes in them, I refused to buy a pair. I had to know that God would provide for me as

He said in His Word. I had to know for myself that God could give me shoes when I needed shoes. Yes, I could have gotten a second job to do that, but I had to know that God would do as He said as long as I did what He told me to do. I would never be able to tell someone that God can supply his needs without having the firsthand experience of God's doing as He promised. No one can ever tell me that anything is impossible for God.

There comes a point in your life when tenacity rises up in you and you make the decision to stay committed to what you've started. You've got to know for yourself that God's Word is true. You've got to know for yourself that God can answer your prayer. I can write book after book and tell you of my experience or the experiences of my family members and others, but it's not the same as your experiencing this truth for yourself. God doesn't want only a select few to witness the joy of having the Word manifested in their lives. He wants this for all His children. So, stop going back to the starting line. Stop bailing out when things become difficult. You may have to put up with some things, but "the sufferings of this present time are not worthy to be compared with the glory which shall be revealed in us" (Rom. 8:18 NKJV). Not only will you get what you've been standing for, but the next time the process will be easier.

As pastor of a large church, I had to know that God would build our new sanctuary debt-free without our having to hold fish fries or rummage sales or sell chicken dinners. Now that I know what God has done for us with that building, the others will be a piece of cake. I have deposited inside me the thrill of victory instead of the torment of defeat.

The next time you sit down to read your Bible, ask yourself if you have experienced what you read or if you are still in the theoretical stage. How many times have you taken the same test?

Giving works, but you're not giving enough for it to work. You haven't been consistent enough for it to work. Kindness or love works, but you haven't been showing it long enough. The Word should be working in your life. Stop wasting time trying to find reasons *why* it's not working and spend more time testifying to folks about how well it does work.

Can't you see what the devil is trying to do? He doesn't want you to have this experience of victory. If he can keep you from having this success, he can keep you bound to him. If he can make you think that the Word doesn't work, he can keep you confused and in doubt.

What happens is this: if you ever get in the middle of something and then don't complete it, you come out with more questions than you had when you started. You come out with more potential to doubt and more potential to find a reason to justify why you couldn't complete the course.

I got tired of hearing about the Word and how it can remove burdens and destroy yokes. I had to make sure that my burdens and yokes were taken out of my way. I've ministered during numerous meetings where there have been miraculous healings and deliverances. The devil regrets the day that I experienced the removal of one burden. Once I saw the first one go, the Holy Spirit inside me said, "You've got the deposit. Now go forth."

Today is the day for you to begin your personal quest for this deposit of victory, and when you get it, nothing will ever be able to stop you. The commitment has to come at the beginning and at the end. Jesus was committed to come to earth to die. He was born to die and He knew that, so He had to be committed from the start. Jesus is the Alpha and the Omega, the beginning and the end. Nothing, not even sweating drops of blood in the Garden of Gethsemane—not even the terrible agony—kept Him from continuing in what He was called to do. He knew that if He stayed true to the law of breakthrough, He would experience the Resurrection. And once He had that experience, every born-again believer could take hold of the same experience of being brought from the death of sin to the life of salvation.

You'll never be the same again. Every time you think about coming off the Word you're standing on, you won't be able to quit. Once that experience is recorded in your spirit, you'll keep going, no matter what.

Look at John 8:31–32: "Then said Jesus to those Jews which believed on him, If ye continue in my word, then are ye my disciples indeed; and ye shall know the truth, and the truth shall make you free." Notice that He said, "If ye continue." Not if you start or if you do it every now and then, but if you continue. When you do this, Jesus said that you are one of the disciplined ones, or one of His disciples. That's how you become disciplined. You start something and keep doing it over and over again. But discipline is not the only thing you'll get from continuing in the Word.

The truth shall make you free. The Word is the truth. You know about the truth, but you must go beyond the written truth to experiencing truth. You must know the truth about the truth. The truth about the truth is the experience of victory.

There is a difference between fact and truth. It may be a fact that you have cancer. But the truth of the Word says, "By [His] stripes you were healed" (1 Peter 2:24 NKJV).

You need to know the truth about the truth. Stand on the Word on healing until you are healed. When you are healed, you not only have the truth, but you also have the truth about the truth. Now you can see your facts changed because you stood on the truth: "But continue thou in the things which thou hast learned and hast been assured of, knowing of whom thou hast learned them" (2 Tim. 3:14).

You've been taught, and you've learned what you're supposed to learn. Allow the law of breakthrough to operate in your life by going all the way with what you've been taught in the Word. Understand that continuance in the Word will produce in your life. Breakthrough is bound to happen when you make the decision to be consistent. When you're tempted to quit, say out loud, "In Jesus' name, I refuse to bail out until I experience victory."

CHAPTER 9

STEP 8:
RECOGNIZE THE DIFFERENCE
BETWEEN MULTIPLIED SEED
AND HARVEST

~~~

He that ministereth seed to the sower both minister bread
for your food, and multiply your seed sown, and increase
the fruits of your righteousness.

(2 COR. 9:10)

Pay close attention to Step 8, and you'll have a greater under-standing of what happens to your seed once it's sown. This is an area in which the devil wants you to be confused because he knows that the finances you sow will bring the promises of God directly to you.

When you plant a seed, two things will come forth: a harvest and more seeds. If you plant corn seed, you will get a harvest of corn, but you'll also get a harvest of corn seed. It's vital that you know the difference between a harvest that is additional seed and a harvest that is the thing you've been expecting and believing God for.

Here's an example of what I mean. Say you're believing God for a house and you plant an initial seed of $20 toward the harvest of your house. You need $5,000 for a down payment before you can even begin negotiations, but for now you have only the $20 seed. You start sowing where you are, and from that initial seed you get $500 back in the form of a bonus from your job. Is that harvest, or is that multiplied seed? It is multiplied seed. Why? Because it's not nearly enough to do what you want to do and that is to put a down payment on your house.

But this is what most folks do. They're so happy they got something back, they're ready to celebrate, having completely forgotten about the goal that started this sowing in the first place. They completely forget that they're believing God for a house.

If a farmer planted two corn seeds, he'll get his harvest of corn, but he'll also get his seed. This farmer wants to go into the corn business. What do you recommend for him to do once he gets that harvest of corn from those two seeds? The correct recommendation, of course, is to plant it so that more corn will come and continue to plant it so that he will reach his goal of having enough corn to go into business.

If he plants those two seeds, but cooks the corn when it comes up, he can forget about his dream of opening up a roadside stand. Once he does that, he will have eaten his seed. Don't laugh. That's what most of us do with our goals. We see a return on our planting, and we get carried away. We feel compelled to do something with it. Anything. "I'll give the church $100, but I'll spend the rest on myself."

That's why the chapter on commitment is so important. You have to see this thing through until the end. You can't stop at $500 when you need $5,000 for your house. You have to keep planting until you receive what you're believing God for.

Now I see why the Bible says to forsake not the assembling of yourselves together with other believers (Heb. 10:25). It's a lot easier for God to meet your needs when you're surrounded by people who believe the same way you believe. Do you think God wants you to go to church just to give the preacher an audience? He wants to help you. Each of us begins to release seeds and to believe God in certain areas, and we assemble ourselves together in the right place. Often, in the place of assembly, God has spoken to someone in prayer about how to get his needs met by meeting your need.

It's easier to meet the needs of the saints when they're gathered together with others who are believing God too. He'll meet your needs sooner in church than He would if you were assembled with others in a nightclub somewhere. I say that because I know that some of you still go to clubs and some even fornicate. Prayerfully, you're reading this book so that the burden-removing, yoke-destroying power can show up in your life and deliver you from the bondage of sin.

Even though answers to dilemmas are being given in this book, some readers will continue to operate the same way they've been operating while expecting different results. You must change. How can things improve and be different if you're doing the same things you've been doing all along?

This even works in relationships. If a man has a wife with a Jezebel spirit—you know, a woman who will curse him out whenever she feels like it—he really needs to follow these steps. Especially if his wife will tell him off in front of his mama. Some mean women like that call themselves Christians. And some men make the mistake of marrying them.

God didn't give me a wife like that because He knew I didn't want to have a jailhouse ministry. He knew exactly what I needed. The Lord knows exactly what you can bear, and He knew I couldn't bear a woman with a Jezebel spirit. I couldn't have a wife who would even think of letting language like that come out of her mouth.

Nobody knows how this type of wife really is but her husband because she doesn't get truly beside herself until she is at home. In public she is sweet and agreeable, but in their house she acts as if she is ready to do him bodily harm. Her mother doesn't even want her around, and that's pretty bad.

But glory to God, there is hope, even for this type of wife. Start sowing seeds now for her to change. Don't wait until she decides to be different. Bring her flowers and watch her attitude change. She'll think that it's such a nice gesture, she'll cook your favorite meal. Okay, now tell me. Is that seed harvest or multiplied seed? That's one dinner, and now is not the time to settle. You need to go all the way.

Capitalize on the seed you've sown. Take that multiplied seed and replant it. Send her a card just for cooking your favorite meal. For that, she'll want to show you much affection when you come home from work. That's more seed. She hasn't completely changed yet.

Don't stop there. Do something romantic. Turn on the hot water in the bathroom, get the mirrors all steamed up, and leave her a love note in the mirror.

If her car is dirty, scribble a note in the dirt on her car. You're adding more seed. You keep going until she becomes so sweet that you can rebuke the Jezebel spirit out of her, just like that.

If you're waiting for your spouse to change, and you're not going to change and do whatever is necessary to open up the door for that change, you'll be waiting a long time. I used to look at my wife and wonder what was wrong with her, and she would give me the same look. I asked God what was wrong with the woman He gave me. I didn't understand anything about her. I went to God and asked Him to change Taffi. He said that He would, just as soon as I changed.

Since then, both of us have tapped into the true definition of submission—don't ask me to do something you're not willing to do. You see, my wife had a problem with the submission thing. She wasn't willing to get married until we found out what the Bible had to say on the matter. We found the verse about "submitting yourselves one to another" (Eph. 5:21). It means to obey, and I couldn't figure out how we were supposed to obey each other.

We found out that our obedience was to God's Word more than it was to each other, so that's what we began to do. We submitted to God's Word, and that submission began to benefit both of us. She changed, I changed, and before we knew it, we were laughing at things that used to cause conflicts in our marriage.

For example, we went three days without speaking to each other. There was no one in the house but us, and we weren't talking. We knew then that there was a definite need for change in our marriage if it was to survive. Once you make the commitment to marry, you need to make the commitment to change.

Continue to plant your seed until you reach the destination that the Word of God has promised. Don't eat your seed. Keep sowing. God wants you to live a prosperous life and to be in a position where the devil will never be able to prevent you from reaching your expected end.

Decide now that you're not going to be the same person you were when you first picked up this book. No matter how good you think you are, you can stand improvement. Everyone can. Decide to have your personal experience of success in the things of God. Commit yourself to His way, and know from this moment forward that you've been changed.

CHAPTER 10

STEP 9:
ACT AS IF IT'S SO

I'm so excited about sharing this message on prosperity that I feel as if I've been born again—again. I can't help this excitement because it seems that everywhere I go, the blessings of God are following me.

There is a difference between a blessing and a miracle. A miracle works in a crisis, and a blessing is perpetual. Blessings don't have to come and go. They're always on the increase and will go down to your children's children. God usually performs miracles when you're in a crisis situation. But when you consistently do what you're supposed to do, He blesses what you're doing, and even your children can take advantage of what you've done.

I prefer to go from blessing to blessing rather than from miracle to miracle. I thank God for miracles because folks sometimes find themselves in crisis situations, but I want to know God's ways and know how to get things to happen on purpose. The Lord told me that instead of expecting a miracle, I should *be* a miracle in someone's life. I'm walking in blessings so that I can be a miracle to others until they learn how to walk in these blessings for themselves.

Prosperity comes about when you're blessed to handle whatever situations come day by day and month by month, without needing to have a miracle show up and bail you out. Miracles are good, but they're not God's best.

Remember the young boy in the Bible who sowed the fish and bread that fed more than five thousand people? That wasn't a miracle; that was a blessing. God blessed his sowing. If he had not sown, the people could not have eaten.

You should know by now that you reap what you sow. If you want to reap prosperity in your life, you must stop acting in ways that oppose your prosperity. You have to change your posture and position and act as if your prosperity is so. That is Step 9.

I meet many people who want to prosper, but they don't act as if they want to prosper. They talk as if they're poor and act as if they're poor and defeated. They hang around defeated people and do things that defeat their own purposes. Then they go to church on Sunday and ask the Lord to prosper them.

If you want prosperity, you'll have to change your posture because God acts like a pitcher. He is ready to throw the ball, but you as the catcher are not in place to receive the pitch. And so, God sits there with your blessing and your prosperity until you position yourself to receive. Once you get in place, God winds up and releases prosperity toward you. Some of you are standing behind the plate saying, "God, throw it. Let me have it!" He can't throw it to you now because if He did, it would hurt you.

This step is so important because it's a step of faith. It requires you to act as if your prosperity is so now and not wait until you see it. Even in the Bible, men and women of God prospered only after they made decisions to act as if the Word of God said they were prosperous.

If the Bible says you're more than a conqueror, begin to act as if it's so. Even if in actuality you're losing, get away from the reality of the world, and jump into the reality of the Word. This Word is more real and more possible than the things you face in the physical world.

This is a faith move that says, I'm doing all the things I know to do to become prosperous, so now I'll act as if it has already happened. This step requires you to change the way you talk and even the way you dress. You can't walk around wearing that same old polyester dress and shopping at Thrift Town. Even if you go to the local upscale department store once a year when it has a 50 percent off sale and you buy something originally expensive but marked down, you don't have to tell others how much you paid for it. That's between you and God. Tell them, "Look what the Lord has done for me."

Go to the fragrance store, and buy samples. Men, stop wearing that supermarket cologne, and get the real deal, even if it's a small bottle.

Don't be offended. You might not see anything wrong with buying cheap stuff, but as long as you do that, you will have a discount mentality. If you are ever going to receive God's best, you're going to have to break through your wall of containment and think big.

I didn't say for you to start acting foolishly and do something without wisdom, such as buy something your pockets cannot presently handle. I'm not telling you to buy a Mercedes when a Toyota is more in line with what is currently manifested in your checking account. I'm telling you to find a Mercedes that you can buy for the price of a Toyota. If it's in bad condition, repair it, wax it, and drive it like the luxury car that it is. Begin to act prosperous, and that's what you'll end up being.

Until you can afford real diamonds, buy cubic zirconias. You can't talk like someone who doesn't have anything. I don't care what you do for a living or where you live. If your home is presently in the projects, no problem. Clean the walls, wax the floor, and make that place sparkle. Something happens when you take care of what you already have. You pass the law of being faithful over a few, and then God will make you the ruler over many. But He won't allow you to rule over much if you aren't even taking care of what you already have.

If you're wondering why you're still where you are, maybe you haven't taken care of what you are presently responsible for. In that case, God cannot bless you with more until you are faithful with what you have. Posture yourself; put yourself in position for God to give you the anointing to cause things to happen that may not be reality yet.

> They came to Jericho: and as he went out of Jericho with his disciples and a great number of people, blind Bartimaeus, the son of Timaeus, sat by the highway side begging. And when he heard that it was Jesus of Nazareth, he began to cry out, and say, Jesus, thou son of David, have mercy on me. And many charged him that he should hold his peace: but he cried the more a great deal, Thou son of David, have mercy on me. And Jesus stood still, and commanded him to be called. (Mark 10:46–49)

What we have here is a fellow who learned of Jesus' presence and started screaming for Jesus to have mercy on him. The folks around him told him to be quiet, which was easy for them to say, since they had their sight. The man was desperate. And the Bible says he cried even louder after they tried to quiet him.

After Jesus acknowledged Bartimaeus and told him to come to Him, everyone's attitude changed: "And they call the blind man, saying unto him, Be of good comfort, rise; he calleth thee. And he, casting away his garment, rose, and came to Jesus" (Mark 10:49–50).

Bartimaeus cast off his garment. He changed his posture and his position, according to biblical terms. The significance of casting away his garment is that the garment told all who passed that he was a blind man. So, Bartimaeus threw away the thing that identified him as something he didn't want to be. I'm getting used to defining things the way the Word defines them, and this is what Bartimaeus's actions conveyed——I'm acting as if I can see, and people who can see don't wear this garment.

Look what happened: "And Jesus answered and said unto him, What wilt thou that I should do unto thee?" (Mark 10:51). Jesus could do something. If Bartimaeus had shown up wearing that blind man's garment, it would have indicated to Jesus that he was not quite ready to receive. Many times we Christians show up before God wearing our old garments—garments of debt, pain, problems, and lack. Instead, try taking off that old thing, and come to Him ready to accept all that He holds for you in His hands.

"The blind man said unto him, Lord, that I might receive my sight. And Jesus said unto him, Go thy way; thy faith hath made thee whole" (Mark 10:51–52). This man changed his whole posture and got into position. That gives yet another definition of faith. How do you know if your faith is working? If you haven't changed your posture, you have not yet begun to operate in faith.

One of the first movements of faith is to put yourself in position as if you're preparing to get something from the Lord.

"Immediately he received his sight, and followed Jesus in the way" (Mark 10:52). Friend, I believe that prosperity can occur in your life immediately if you'll change your posture and position. He cannot give you the anointing to prosper when you're still acting as if you're waiting for it to happen. You have to behave as if it's already so.

I can remember when our church was located in a school cafeteria, and we had only eight members. Instead of leaving the cafeteria tables out, we set things up as if we were a big church. We put chairs on each side of the cafeteria and made a middle aisle. We put up a banner and got some plants to make it look as though we were having a crusade every Sunday. We were acting as if it were so. God didn't give me a vision of a little church, so we had to stop acting like one. We even changed the words to "This Little Light of Mine" and started singing about this *big* light of mine. Did it make a difference? Absolutely.

If I'm expecting what I pray for to manifest, I have to change my attitude and my placement in order to get what I desire. Look at Mark 2:2–4:

> Straightway many were gathered together, insomuch that there was no room to receive them, no, not so much as about the door: and he preached the word unto them. And they come unto him, bringing one sick of the palsy, which was borne of four. And when they could not come nigh unto him for the press, they uncovered the roof where he was: and when they had broken it up, they let down the bed wherein the sick of the palsy lay.

Tearing up someone's roof is a desperate move. But look at verse 9: "Whether is it easier to say to the sick of the palsy, Thy sins be forgiven thee; or to say, Arise, and take up thy bed, and walk?"

Is it easier to say, "Change your posture and position"? Notice what He meant when He said, "Arise." Instead of lying on that bed, instead of that bed carrying you, change your position and carry the bed: "But that ye may know that the Son of man hath power on earth to forgive sins, (he saith to the sick of the palsy,) I say unto thee, Arise, and take up thy bed, and go thy way into thine house. And immediately he arose" (Mark 2:10–12). Jesus was telling him to put himself in a place for Jesus to release anointing to bring what he was seeking to pass.

You may be asking yourself why it's necessary for you to act as if it's so. Luke 7:12–16 is the story about the widow who lost her only son. Jesus interrupted the funeral procession.

> Now when he came nigh to the gate of the city, behold, there was a dead man carried out, the only son of his mother, and she was a widow: and much people of the city was with her. And when the Lord saw her, he had compassion on her, and said unto her, Weep not. And he came and touched the bier: and they that bare him stood still. And he said, Young man, I say unto thee, Arise.

Change your posture and your position. This must be a key element to prosperity if Jesus keeps requesting it, even when someone is dead: "And he that was dead sat up, and began to speak" (Luke 7:15). Now, that's a change. He did the opposite of what dead men usually do: "And he delivered him to his mother. And there came a fear on all: and they glorified God, saying,

That a great prophet is risen up among us; and, That God hath visited his people" (Luke 7:15–16).

You can't continue to operate in tradition, doubt, and unbelief and expect the glory of God to visit your house: "Arise, shine; for thy light is come, and the glory of the LORD is risen upon thee" (Isa. 60:1). You must be in position before the glory can be in position to bring blessings into your life: "For, behold, the darkness shall cover the earth, and gross darkness the people: but the LORD shall arise upon thee, and his glory shall be seen upon thee" (Isa. 60:2).

When will all this happen? When you change. When you start speaking faith. When you start acting as if it's so. When you start saying no to sin. Then the glory, the prosperity, and the anointing of God will change faith's posture and position. Instead of being dormant inside you, faith will activate and start producing good things in your life.

> Lift up thine eyes round about, and see: all they gather themselves together, they come to thee: thy sons shall come from far, and thy daughters shall be nursed at thy side. Then thou shalt see, and flow together, and thine heart shall fear, and be enlarged; because the abundance of the sea shall be converted unto thee, the forces of the Gentiles shall come unto thee. (Isa. 60:4–5)

Forces means "wealth." Wealth will come to change your status. Prosperity will invade your life when you change the way you're standing, the way you're looking at your situation.

I need to answer the question about why you should act as if it's so. I know that you can look pretty foolish behaving in that way. I know Jesus did, especially when He was talking to that fig tree. He said that no man would ever eat the fruit of that tree thereafter, and the disciples heard Him say that. Then He went His way as if it had already happened (Matt. 21:19).

Is it vital as a Christian that I start acting as if something has already occurred? Walking, talking, and conducting myself as if it had already come to pass?

I heard someone say once that you can't fool God. But you know, we're not trying to fool God; we're trying to fool the devil. The Bible has already told us that God is not mocked, so we know that we can't fool Him, and we shouldn't try to (Gal. 6:7).

Follow me closely here, and look at 1 John 2:15–17:

> Love not the world, neither the things that are in the world. If any man love the world, the love of the Father is not in him. For all that is in the world, the lust of the flesh, and the lust of the eyes, and the pride of life, is not of the Father, but is of the world. And the world passeth away, and the lust thereof: but he that doeth the will of God abideth for ever.

Don't love the world. Don't love the system, operation, or things of this world. When the Bible uses this term, it's not referring to the planet earth. When you see the word *world* in the New Testament, it's talking about a system of operation of which Satan is in charge, the lust-filled system that operates according to demonic standards.

The world is going to pass away, along with the lusts of the world. But he that does God's will abides forever. At that time, sin will no longer be a problem. Because of the blood of Jesus, the problem of sin is taken care of. Sin was dealt with when Jesus was on the cross. So, your sin is not the devil's business; it's God's business. When you sin, it's not an unsolvable problem because as a Christian, you have the blood of Jesus.

In God, you have the solution to sin. God knew about whatever you've done that doesn't line up with His Word before you even confessed your transgression. Go to the Lord and say, "I did it." He already knows what you did. The angels were there to take a record of it.

Imagine that every time you sin, an angel is sitting right in your face. When you get to heaven, you can't lie about what you've done because your angels were taking notes. The room you're in right now is filled with angels watching over you. One day you'll find out just what was around you the whole time. Imagine, when you light up a cigarette, you're blowing smoke in an angel's face. It's kind of hard to sin when you get the revelation that someone is watching you.

I was walking down the hall of our house one day. No one was home but me. I passed by my daughter's room, and I heard a voice say, "Somebody loves you." I backed toward the door, and I heard it again. I'm thinking, *God is trying to talk to me through a bear.* Nothing is impossible for Him, you know.

When my wife and daughters got home, I told them I believed that God loved me so much, He was trying to tell me through the bear. My daughter said, "No, Daddy. Squeeze it. It talks." Even though I was wrong that time, I'm right about the angels. I'm always aware that someone is around me. That's why repentance is necessary.

The sower soweth the word. And these are they by the way side, where the word is sown; but when they have heard, Satan cometh immediately, and taketh away the word that was sown in their hearts. And these are they likewise which are sown on stony ground; who, when they have heard the word, immediately receive it with gladness; and have no root in themselves, and so endure but for a time: afterward, when affliction or persecution ariseth for the word's sake, immediately they are offended. And these are they which are sown among thorns; such as hear the word, and the cares of this world, and the deceitfulness of riches, and the lusts of other things entering in, choke the word, and it becometh unfruitful. (Mark 4:14–19)

The devil is after the Word. He doesn't ever want you to get the Word. And he'll do whatever he needs to do to stop you from getting the Word because it is the principal thing. He doesn't care if you die and go to heaven; he wants you out of the way. Trouble, affliction, persecution, lust, and the cares of this world are all forms of pressure.

You may see them as problems, but they represent pressure. Lust, for example, is pressure applied to your flesh. When the cares of the world come in, that's pressure to get you off the Word. Satan tries to achieve results by applying pressure. He tries to get you to walk in sin and have his word come to pass in your life by applying pressure.

When you sin, you can repent, and it's over with. But have you ever noticed that right after you repent of your sin, more pressure comes to try to throw you off course? What's pressuring you right now? There are pressures from your past, pressures from yesterday, pressures from last week; something is always pressing in on you to try to keep you from reaching the final result. Satan wants to bring his word to pass in your life, and he uses pressure to do it.

If you don't understand anything else, understand this:

nothing just happens, whether it's positive or negative. Prosperity doesn't just happen; neither does sin. You don't just jump into bed with someone you're not married to. Pressure had to come to you from somewhere. And if the pressure stays on you, and you continue to be pressed, you end up back in the same problem Jesus has already solved, which is sin.

Focusing on this passage for a moment, notice the words that are italicized: "Brethren, I count not myself to have apprehended: but *this* one thing *I do,* forgetting those things which are behind, and reaching forth unto those things which are before, I press toward the mark for the prize of the high calling of God in Christ Jesus" (Phil. 3:13–14). Translators have added these words for emphasis or clarification.

When you drop them, it reads like this: "Brethren, I count not myself to have apprehended but one thing." Paul said, "I've not captured or apprehended but one thing. I've got this one thing. I've captured this one thing, and that is to forget the things that are behind me."

Child of God, if you don't forget the things that are behind you, they will add to your pressure. You forget the things that are behind you because to remember them will only put more pressure on your life.

If you've been watching pornography all week, you'd better let it go when you repent. If you don't, it's going to cause more pressure. Your past is designed to pressure you. That's why the devil always brings up your past because it's a way for him to add pressure. The Bible calls him the accuser of the brethren (Rev. 12:10). He is always digging back into yesterday to accuse you and pressure you today. That is what lust is, pressure.

Now, you have a choice. You have what's before you, and you have what's behind you. The things behind you are pressing you, and the things before you are potential blessings. Just act as if the things before you from the Word of God are supposed to happen.

Paul said that he was no longer going to let his past pressure him. He decided to start putting pressure on the Word. That's what you are to do instead of allowing Satan to pressure you; you pressure him with the Word of God. Let him see what it feels like. Every morning when you get up, start praying in tongues. Every time someone looks around, he should find you speaking the Word of God.

When the devil tries to pressure you about your past, take the Word, and place the pressure on him where it rightfully belongs. When he says you'll never prosper, tell him in the name of Jesus that prosperity is yours. When you praise God and call on the name of Jesus in the midst of your trials, that's more pressure than the old devil can bear. Keep it up, and it will get to the point that when you wake up in the morning, he'll say, "Oh, no, she's up again."

"Therefore I say unto you, What things soever ye desire, when ye pray, believe that ye receive them, and ye shall have them" (Mark 11:24). After you've finished praying, act as if it's so, and you shall have what you prayed for. Do you see how you're the one applying the pressure here? When I stand praying and believe that I have what I've prayed for, I'm putting the pressure on. I'm putting pressure on the devil, who is trying to pressure me in the other direction.

When you believe you've received, you're acting as if you already have what you prayed for. You're putting faith pressure on the Word of God and feeling less and less of the pressure that Satan is trying to apply. The pressure to sin decreases when you apply the pressure to operate in righteousness. So, press.

Press your way into the anointing of God. Don't accept pressure to get drunk. But put pressure on getting drunk in the Holy Spirit.

You're in the middle. It's either press or be pressed. Make up your mind to change your posture and position, and press the devil right out of your life. Treat the Bible as a script, and act out the Word of God. Put pressure on the forces of the unseen spiritual world so that something can break through to this physical world. As you put pressure on the Word for healing, it begins to travel through the realm of the spirit until it gets to the door of the natural realm and into reality. Faith causes your healing to manifest.

I have the perfect example to share with you. For at least seven years I had been telling everyone who would listen that one day I'd speak at one of Kenneth Copeland Ministries' Believer's Conventions. I prayed that they would understand that God called me to be a part of that team. I diligently prayed for everyone involved in the convention. And when I first started saying that, my wife laughed at me and said I was hallucinating.

The first time I spoke at the Believer's Convention, the anointing was so strong that Brother Copeland ran out to the car and asked if I could speak at all of the conventions until Jesus comes. He said they all took a vote, and it was unanimous. Jesse Duplantis told him that he should have asked me years ago.

To someone on the outside, it appears as if that just happened. But nothing just happens. For years I've been pressing and pressing, and it finally broke through to the physical realm. I applied the same type of pressure to the prosperity that my ministry is walking in today. That's how we built the Dome and acquired the adjacent shopping center property. I told my members to thank God for our new property every time they drove past that location. Today, our outreach departments are housed on that very spot.

And to think that some of you sit at home, not opening your mouths, not reading the Word, or not putting pressure on the Word, and you expect God to respond. Nothing has changed in your life because you haven't pressed the issue.

If you're tired of living where you're living, press the issue with God. Let Him know that you're not going to stop bugging Him until you get what He promises in His Word. Every time you get in a conversation, say what you want to see. Keep the pressure on, and don't let anything come out of your mouth to disrupt things. Have you ever blown up one of those big balloons? What happens when you take the pressure off and stop blowing? All the work you've put in is lost and the balloon deflates. Eventually, the spiritual balloon is going to pop, and your prosperity will be coming from every direction.

It's time to press the devil out of your life, your finances, your marriage, and your body. When I act as if it's so, I'm applying pressure on the Word for the reality to manifest.

Understand that the pressure is not on you for God's Word to come to pass; it's all on God. Since you're not the one who said that by the stripes of Jesus you're healed, the pressure for healing doesn't belong to you. That's how I resolve nervousness now. When I stood before thousands of people as I did at the Believer's Convention, I reminded God that I didn't call all those folks there; He did. And since He called them there, He was the One responsible for slowing down my racing heart.

I had to keep telling myself that there weren't that many people in the arena. Every time I looked up, though, my heart was beating just as fast. *No problem. No problem. I preach to this many people every week,* I told myself. When I finally decided to step off the podium and get down where they were sitting, I felt better. Healing broke loose throughout the convention. The pressure had been applied, and the anointing took charge.

Whatever you're believing God for, put as much pressure on it as you can. Write a note and put it on the refrigerator with the appropriate Scripture on it. Put the Word about what you desire in your mouth and in your heart. The Bible says, don't let the Word of God depart from out of your mouth (Josh. 1:8). Keep saying it. The Bible says to keep and guard it in your heart, for out of it flow the issues of life (Prov. 4:23).

Say no to negative pressure, but say yes to God. If you can't seem to find enough time to keep the Word of God in front of your eyes because you're busy watching other things, don't expect to receive what you've prayed for. No pressure is applied in that instance. You have to be consistent and committed about this. It's not considered pressure when you pray only once a week. You can't press unless there is something coming against you. Be aware that there will be some devilish things coming your way. When you press into the Word, you win.

I know what God means when He admonishes us not to be slothful. A slothful man isn't consistent enough to build up any pressure to receive anything from God.

If the doctor told me I was going to die, I wouldn't get in the Word on healing every now and then. I'd do it constantly. If I'm fighting for my life, I'm not going to waste two hours and watch soap operas and funny videos. I don't have time for that, and neither do you when the medical report says you don't have long to live. Put the pressure on your healing.

Some people might consider this idea fanatical, but one day you're going to be fanatically prosperous in every area of your life. Then, of course, they'll think it was good fortune, but you know that it was pressure.

Everything I have right now in my life is the result of faith pressure. Even Taffi. I put pressure on the Word and got the wife of my dreams. I reminded God that He said I could have the desires of my heart, and I described her to a tee. I got exactly what I wanted.

A lot of folks think she and I are prosperous because we pastor a big church, but what they don't know is that we were prosperous long before the church reached the size it is today. We would prosper if you put us in the middle of a ghetto because we know how to press.

Get your Bible and concordance, and make a list of verses that correspond to what you're standing on. Apply that faith pressure to the Word, act as if it's so, and expect the reality. Nothing just happens!

CHAPTER 11

STEP 10:
OBEY GOD'S WORD

$\sim$

If you love Me, keep My commandments.

(JOHN 14:15 NKJV)

You know the old saying that talk is cheap. It's not enough for you to say that you love the Lord. No, that's not nearly enough. Jesus let His disciples know that they could prove their love for Him by doing the things that He commanded. "If you love Me," He told them, "then you'll do whatever I tell you to do."

I want you to recognize, however, that you can't do what God tells you to do if you don't know what He is telling you to do. If you're not spending time in the Word or if you go to church only once a month, it will be difficult for you to know what He is saying. Therefore, I submit to you that the degree of your love for the Father is going to be enhanced by what you know or limited by what you don't know.

When I was first born again, I was accustomed to doing some things that I truly did not know were sinful, so even after giving my life to Christ, I continued to do those things. Eventually, I came to a place of understanding the sin in which I was operating, but prior to that, I was operating based on my limited knowledge of the Word.

Until you spend time in the Word on a regular basis, you're not going to be able to love God to a high degree. You can't obey God in areas in which you lack knowledge. Step 10 is about obeying God's Word.

In the book of Job, we find that when a man is not obeying God's Word and he is not getting in the Word so that he can obey God, his prosperity will be affected: "If they obey and serve him, they shall spend their days in prosperity, and their years in pleasures" (36:11).

Would you like to experience this? God makes it very simple for you. He says that if you obey and serve, you shall be prosperous. He has connected obedience with servanthood in this verse. You cannot obey God and fail to serve Him because the two are tied together. You can't go to church and serve the pastor if you're not obeying God.

If you obey Him, God will make sure that you're in control of whatever your hands touch. If you begin to walk in obedience to His Word, His promise is that no matter what happens to you in life, no matter where you end up, He is going to cause you to prosper. I like the part about spending your years "in pleasures." I like that because not many of us realize that God wants us to have pleasures.

Someone says, "Well, what kind of pleasures does He mean?" Driving the car you've always wanted to drive, that's pleasurable, isn't it? Being healthy and being full of joy sound like pleasure to me. And how about not having a nagging wife or a lazy husband? God will see to it that your life is spent in pleasure. Glory to God!

Maybe the problems you're experiencing right now are related to the area of obedience. Maybe you're picking and choosing what you want to obey in God's Word instead of doing what God has told you to do.

If you wouldn't think of committing adultery but also wouldn't think of tithing, you're not obeying all that God has commanded you (Ex. 20:14; Mal. 3:10). You can't say that you'll do one part of the Bible but not another if you truly love God. This is not a fast-food restaurant where you can have it your way. You will have to do it God's way if you want to benefit from the ways of God. Since this is something that will affect your prosperity in particular and your salvation in general, you need to make a quality decision to do all that the Lord commands you to do.

To put it in plain and simple language, you must obey God. Don't expect anything from Him if you're not doing what He says. Any parent can attest to that. A teenager comes to the parent and asks for money to buy a car. As a parent, you will not be inclined or motivated to do anything for a disobedient teen. Yet as a Christian, you will disobey God and expect Him to heal you when you ask, pay the overdue light bill, and deliver you from the bondage you got yourself into in the first place. You're in a covenant relationship with the Lord that says He'll do for you if you do for Him.

Conversely, if you don't do anything for Him, He won't do anything for you. If you forgive others, then God can forgive you (Mark 11:25–26). If you don't forgive others, God can't forgive you. It works the same way with obedience. God is receptive to those who are receptive to His will and His way. To behave otherwise hinders the prosperity God is trying to bring to your life: "Behold, I set before you this day a blessing and a curse; a blessing, if ye obey the commandments of the LORD your God, which I command you this day" (Deut. 11:26–27).

The blessing is based on whether or not you will obey what the Lord has told you. I want to remind you, however, that you cannot obey what you don't know to do, and you're never going to know what to do if you don't read the Word or assemble with other believers. These two activities are vital to your success.

We learn from the book of Deuteronomy, "And shalt return unto the LORD thy God, and shalt obey his voice according to all that I command thee this day, thou and thy children, with all thine heart, and with all thy soul" (Deut. 30:2). He admonished us not only to obey the Word, but also to teach our children how to obey the Word of God.

> Thou shalt return and obey the voice of the LORD, and do all his commandments which I command thee this day. And the LORD thy God will make thee plenteous in every work of thine hand, in the fruit of thy body, and in the fruit of thy cattle, and in the fruit of thy land, for good: for the LORD will again rejoice over thee for good, as he rejoiced over thy fathers. (Deut. 30:8–9)

Child of God, all you have to do is to obey His commandments and He promises to make you plenteous and successful in every work of your hand. Everything will prosper in your hand if you'll begin to obey. In so doing, you will have to come away from the pressures the world puts on you to compromise your convictions and the Word of God. You will have to make up your mind to serve either the world or God because you cannot serve both.

I'm sure there are some of you who can attest to the fact that the world will let you down at the very time you feel you need to rely on the world system the most. God said He would never leave you or forsake you; He will always be there when you need Him (Heb. 13:5).

By now you should understand fully how obedience will enhance your prosperity and disobedience will hinder your prosperity. But I want you to understand something in addition to this. You cannot hang around people who disobey God's Word and be deceived into thinking that their behavior won't in some way rub off on you. It's not possible to be in the company of folks who are sinning all the time and doing things contrary to God and expect that this anti-anointing will not affect you.

As Christians, we so often feel that someone else's sin is not our business, but it absolutely is our business. The born-again person who continues to sin is a part of the same body of Christ to which you and I belong. I don't want him to affect the whole house. I can't associate with disobedient Christians. I'm not talking about sinners. I'm talking about people who are saved but disobey God's Word. Hear me when I say that if you do this, it won't be long before you start considering doing some of the same things. I get excited when I can bring words of wisdom from God that will bring about change in your life. Staying on my face in the presence of the Lord allows my spiritual antenna to search out areas I need to focus on for the sake of the body.

Look at 2 Thessalonians 3:6–15:

> Now we command you, brethren, in the name of our Lord Jesus Christ, that ye withdraw yourselves from every brother that walketh disorderly, and not after the tradition which he received of us. For yourselves know how ye ought to follow us:

for we behaved not ourselves disorderly among you; neither did we eat any man's bread for nought; but wrought with labor and travail night and day, that we might not be chargeable to any of you: not because we have not power, but to make ourselves an example unto you to follow us. For even when we were with you, this we commanded you, that if any would not work, neither should he eat. For we hear that there are some which walk among you disorderly, working not at all, but are busybodies. Now them that are such we command and exhort by our Lord Jesus Christ, that with quietness they work, and eat their own bread. But ye, brethren, be not weary in well doing. And if any man obey not our word by this epistle, note that man, and have no company with him, that he may be ashamed. Yet count him not as an enemy, but admonish him as a brother.

"Now we command you, brethren." It was not a request, and Paul was not making the command to a sinner. He used the word *brethren,* so you know he was talking to people who were born again.

The Amplified Bible puts into perspective how God expects for you to handle the situation when you see a brother not walking according to the Word: "For you yourselves know how it is necessary to imitate our example, for we were not disorderly or shirking of duty when we were with you—we were not idle" (2 Thess. 3:7). Paul said, "Look at our example. We did not shirk or neglect our duties, and we were not idle. We did not eat anyone's bread without paying for it."

That's the description of a freeloader. Some people will use Christianity as an excuse to freeload. Paul said that was not a godly example: "But with toil and struggle we worked night and day, that we might not be a burden or impose on any of you [for our support]" (2 Thess. 3:8 AMPLIFIED).

Some of us have gotten so sophisticated, we actually think we have a right to sit down and not work because the job we want is not available. The Bible speaks against this attitude. You're not to be idle, especially if you're a man with a family and bills to pay. You don't sit back and wait for the job you want to open up when you have responsibilities. You do whatever you have to do.

My dad pumped gas and worked two, sometimes three jobs to take care of his family. And some men sit back and say what they *won't* do to earn a living. Despite the HELP WANTED signs on display in many store windows, they'd rather freeload and use other Christians than apply for those jobs. They need to help themselves and get busy filling out job applications.

I'd do whatever I needed to do to take care of my wife and children. I don't care if it's working in a fast-food restaurant or cutting lawns. Any work that is legal is honorable because you're obeying the Word and taking care of your family.

Nothing is sorrier than a healthy man who lounges at home while his wife is out working to support the family. In the meantime, he sits at home with his pride because he has a degree and doesn't want anyone to see him working in a fast-food restaurant. I'm sure that someone reading this has a problem with what I've just said, but I stand by every word.

God has not created you to be a man so that you can lie around at home while your wife is out taking care of the family. Don't think that I don't know what I'm talking about. I earned a college degree and took a job selling pots and pans from the back of my car until I could find something better. I signed up for substitute teaching and did whatever I could do to make an honest living. I knew God would turn things around for me after a while because my faith was strong.

> [It was] not because we do not have a right [to such support], but [we wished] to make ourselves an example for you to follow. For while we were yet with you, we gave you this rule and charge: If any one would not work, neither let him eat. Indeed, we hear that some among you are disorderly—that they are passing their lives in idleness, neglectful of duty—being busy with other people's affairs instead of their own and doing no work. (2 Thess. 3:9–11 AMPLIFIED)

Paul was talking about people who didn't have jobs, but had enough time to sit back and criticize what someone else was doing. There are actually people who walk around in the manner these verses describe—folks whose lights are turned off, who are about to be evicted, and they still find time to comment on other people's lives.

If you are in that position and have so much time to think about others, try thinking about getting a job and supporting your family, so the church doesn't have to do it.

Don't continue to find excuses to stay where you are. Get up, get out, and get something positive happening in your life. Whatever you do, stop using the sorry excuse that all the jobs are being given to other racial groups and you have to work twice as hard to get ahead. If that's the case, and I don't say that it is, at least you'll be twice as prepared when you get there.

Paul continued, "Now we charge and exhort such persons [as ministers in Him exhorting those] in the Lord Jesus Christ, the Messiah, that they work in quietness and earn their own food and other necessities. And as for you, brethren, do not become weary or lose heart in doing right" (2 Thess. 3:12–13 AMPLIFIED).

While you're associating with these folks, there is a tendency to lose heart to do what you've been taught is right. To safeguard against this happening in my personal life, I won't allow my wife to go around with a woman who is disobedient to her husband or condone her association with a gossiping woman. It may come as a surprise to you that I say that, but I know that whomever she spends time around, she has the potential to bring that spirit back home with her.

It's not a matter of me putting my foot down and demanding that she not befriend these women because with my wife that's not necessary. We sit down and discuss everything, including her friendships. If necessary, I say to her, "Sweetheart, you know this woman is a gossip, she has a Jezebel spirit, she defies her husband's authority, and she disrespects him in front of other people. I don't know if we should be keeping company with her." Neither will my wife allow me to spend time with a man who flirts or is an adulterer because as the Bible says, "Evil communications corrupt good manners" (1 Cor. 15:33).

It is not healthy to your born-again spirit to hook up with people who are behaving disorderly. However, before you disassociate yourself for a time from such people, you should confront them in love to let them know what they're doing wrong and explain how they can get it right.

No matter who you are or what office you hold in your church, you can't hang around with disobedient folks and be deceived into thinking that it won't rub off on you. I will not allow myself to do that.

If someone I know is walking in sin, I guarantee that I will say something to him about it. He is a part of me, and I'm a part of him. The church has to stop turning its back on itself when it sees a part of the body being broken. If the wooden portion of the roof were to confront the shingles, then we wouldn't have a leak affecting the floor, carpet, or atmosphere of the house.

We're all together in the house of God, and if the front door is broken, we need to fix it before the devil bursts through it. The body of Christ would not be in the mess it's in today if we would all do our part. If every joint would supply instead of everyone turning his back, we would be able to come out of this.

If you see a young woman wearing a short, tight, inappropriate dress to church, don't just sit there. You know you're going to make a comment about it when you get home anyway. It won't do her any good then, and besides, gossiping is a sin. Pull her aside, and explain to her in sisterly love how she is to dress now that she has turned her life over to Christ.

When I came out of the world, people had to pull me aside and instruct me on certain things. Otherwise I would not have had a clue. Of course, you need to be tactful when you do this. If it's a matter of someone's dress code, offer to take your new sister in the Lord shopping for clothes that represent her new lifestyle in Jesus. Let her know that what she wears is a form of advertising and that she needs to dress in a way that lets everyone know that she is part of the body of Christ. You have a responsibility to confront disobedience.

The Scripture says that after you have brought such things to a person's attention and he chooses to disobey, you are not to keep company with him. It doesn't say to be a witness to the sin and walk away. If you see the sin, deal with it according to the Word of God, and if the person chooses not to line up with the Word, then don't keep his company. You show him not only your disapproval, but also your commitment toward God. You show that your responsibility to obey God is greater than your relationship with him.

Disconnecting from this person has a way of making him think about the sin he has committed and the repentance that will be necessary for him to get back into right standing with God. If he values God's love and your friendship, it won't be long before things are back in order. It does no good for you to compromise with the sin of others.

Disobedience can hinder your prosperity. On the other hand, obedience welcomes and even increases your wealth in the things of God. Knowledge is directly tied to your ability to obey the Word. When I was born again, I didn't know what fornication was and couldn't pronounce the word. Just like many of you, I thought there was nothing wrong with having sex before marriage. Then I got the Word of God on that subject and others that I was not aware were sinful practices.

Only after I found out what I had been doing wrong could I be obedient to God. I made up my mind to change my life and do whatever God said for me to do. Knowledge of the Word is the basis for your obedience.

People don't behave in the way the Bible commands them because for the most part, they have not been taught to do so. When the word of truth finally comes, they meet it with doubt and unbelief because it is not something they have heard before.

That brings me to the next step. I want to preface the next chapter by saying that it has not been written solely for the benefit of pastors, preachers, and ministers; it is for the benefit of the body. Regardless of whether or not you have heard what you're about to read, it's scriptural and it's true.

This is a small fox that has absolutely stopped prosperity in the lives of many Christians. My objective in this next step is to show you what the Word has to say and then give you an understanding of the information you need in order to be obedient.

CHAPTER 12

STEP 11:
BELIEVE AND TRUST IN YOUR
MAN OF GOD

A n integral step on your way to total-life prosperity is that
you must believe and trust in your man of God—your pastor or spiritual leader. That is Step 11. Let's take a look at what
the Lord has to say on this issue: "They rose early in the morning, and went forth into the wilderness of Tekoa: and as they
went forth, Jehoshaphat stood and said, Hear me, O Judah, and
ye inhabitants of Jerusalem: Believe in the LORD your God, so
shall ye be established; believe his prophets, so shall ye prosper"
(2 Chron. 20:20).

Your prosperity will be based in part on whether you believe
and trust in your man of God. There is a great attack against you
where this is concerned. The attack against you, which causes
you to doubt and mistrust, in turn attacks your prosperity.
Everyone reading this book has experienced someone saying
something ugly about the man of God.

You may be affected by years of past offenses committed by

other pastors, which may cause you to stereotype all men of God. It's almost a subconscious guilty-by-association syndrome, which allows the past to become an enemy of your present and future prosperity. Maybe you had a bad experience in a former church or a bad relationship that you failed to deal with, and you brought it along like excess baggage to your present church home. Your lack of trust for the authority of members in your former place of worship comes back and causes doubt and unbelief for your present man of God, and it hinders rather than helps your spiritual and personal progress.

I want to deal specifically with what you have heard about men of God and money in the church. Let me start by saying that I will not associate with anyone who bad-mouths my man of God, Kenneth Copeland. I won't even stay present when ugly things are being said about him, and I will voice my serious displeasure before I leave the scene.

I discuss this topic with my members because I am the man of God who concerns them the most. We're hooked up together, and rather than talk in generalities, I talk in specifics with them on this subject. I tell them that they're going to hear things said about the preacher stealing money from the church. Ironically, the more prosperous the church and the more people join, the bigger a crook other folks are going to make him out to be.

Since I don't know the particulars of your church, let me explain what happens at our ministry and relate our procedure to biblical doctrine. It is virtually impossible for me to steal money from our church. Ours is not a little church where the preacher can walk into the finance room and say, "Show me the money." It doesn't work like that. The United States government, through the Internal Revenue Service, has set up certain rules and regulations by which we are to conduct ourselves. My salary is handled by a compensation board, consisting of people who are not members of our church or members of my family.

The three members of the compensation board reside out of state. Each year they come together with a lawyer to determine what my salary will be in accordance with specific government guidelines and boundaries. As a means of further protection, no sole individual in our ministry, including my wife, Taffi, and me, can withdraw money or sign a check; multiple signatures are required. I can't go to the bank and say, "My name is Creflo Dollar. Give me one thousand dollars, please." The teller would look at me, smile, and remind me that that's not allowed. And she would probably call our accountant as soon as I left the bank.

Our church has an excellent Harvard graduate accountant who keeps up with every dime that comes in and goes out of the church. As if that's not enough, every year the ministry is audited to ensure that nothing has transpired outside the boundaries.

Our ministry has been given the status of high financial integrity, and our procedures are recommended by the government as a standard to be used in other ministries. Other than my church members and those of you reading this book, no one else has been given that information. Some people mistakenly believe that I can go to the financial department of the church and get money whenever I feel like it. So, folks have come up to some of my members and said things like, "I see from that house he lives in and that car he drives, your pastor is taking all of your money."

Not to defend myself, but to enable my members to trust me,

I had to set the record straight. I told them that in addition to my salary, I receive an honorarium whenever I go somewhere to preach, which is often. How have I managed to prosper this way? I can't help it. I'm doing these 14 steps!

I'm like a farmer who can't help it when he gets a harvest from the seeds he plants in the ground. The system works, and I can say that because I do these steps myself. It works, glory to God!

With all the travel and preaching this ministry is involved in throughout the world, we have been able to supply jobs to people not only in this country, but also in countries abroad. Things like that don't just happen. The prosperity has to start somewhere.

Now, that's the natural side of things. Let's go to the supernatural, spiritual side and see what the Bible has to say about all of this. Put the two together and you'll be able to operate supernaturally to achieve your prosperity.

Every year at our church, we have a pastor's appreciation celebration. The information I'm about to share with you was given as a blessing to my members, so they could understand why it's necessary to have this event each year. They had to be taught, as I'm sure many of you need to be taught, that a celebration of appreciation for your man of God is more for your sake than for his.

The first year we had one, I set up the entire thing because I had to teach everyone how to appreciate me. That may sound comical, but how can you expect people to do things by the Word if someone doesn't instruct them? The Bible says: "Render therefore to all their dues: tribute to whom tribute is due; custom to whom custom; fear to whom fear; honor to whom honor" (Rom. 13:7). And in the Amplified Bible it reads, "Render to all men their dues. [Pay] taxes to whom taxes are due, revenue to whom revenue is due, respect to whom respect is due, and honor to whom honor is due."

If you honor the gift that God has put in your midst in the form of your man of God, He has promised in His Word that He will honor you. It's important that you understand why it is necessary to honor your man of God because people outside your church aren't tied to him as you are and they don't know what they're talking about when they bad-mouth him.

In our church we have an understanding to exercise our faith in all matters to keep fear from hindering our prosperity. We don't want to put our prosperity on the line, and I'm sure you don't want to, either, where your church is concerned. The Bible is very clear about this: "Touch not mine anointed, and do my prophets no harm" (Ps. 105:15). Why do you think the psalmist said that? Because if you become a burden and a yoke in the life of an anointed man called by God, you set yourself up to be removed by the anointing on that person's life.

God will not allow you to get in the way of someone He has appointed to carry out His will after having set that ministry gift into motion to operate at that particular time. If someone comes along and becomes a hindrance to what God has ordained to take place, that someone will have to go. God will not allow His chosen ones to be upset or upstaged by anyone. He would rather remove the burdensome one than remove the one through whom He has chosen to accomplish a certain assignment. I tell my members that if they become a burden to me through strife, gossip, or division, they set themselves up to be dealt with by my Boss, the Almighty. And if He calls you into His office, you'd better watch out.

That's why I don't listen to certain radio programs or read

certain magazines or newspapers. God tells us not to listen to everything or open up our spirits to everything that's being said. If there is something in them that becomes a burden to that man of God, He has to deal with it some way or another. So, it's for the sake of others that I don't allow myself to hear a bunch of junk about myself or my ministry. It's for the sake of the people that I don't open my ears to gossip.

It's the same type of situation that we find in Genesis. Although Moses prayed to God to let Miriam off the hook for what she had said about him, God still struck her with leprosy and removed her from the camp. She was about to hinder the objective that God wanted to accomplish through Moses. It's a very serious thing when He tells you not to touch an anointed one. He doesn't mean walking up and putting your hands on the person. He means touching with your mouth. When you open your mouth against an anointed person of God, you touch him and put yourself in a position to experience a touch from God.

First Timothy 5:17–20 instructs us,

Let the elders that rule well be counted worthy of double honor, especially they who labor in the word and doctrine. For the scripture saith, Thou shalt not muzzle the ox that treadeth out the corn. And, The laborer is worthy of his reward. Against an elder receive not an accusation, but before two or three witnesses. Them that sin rebuke before all, that others also may fear.

The word *elder* is currently used to refer to an older man, but in the New Testament it refers to the office of a pastor. Another word you see in the New Testament is *shepherd, overseer,* or *bishop.* You see the word *pastor* only within the list of the fivefold ministry gifts (Eph. 4:11).

In the Amplified Bible we read,

> Let the elders who perform the duties of their office well be considered doubly worthy of honor [and adequate financial support], especially those who labor faithfully in preaching and teaching. For the Scripture says, You shall not muzzle an ox when it is treading out the grain, and again, The laborer is worthy of his hire. Listen to no accusation preferred [before a judge] against an elder except it be confirmed by the testimony of two or three witnesses. (1 Tim. 5:17–19)

It says here that when people make an accusation against your man of God, you're not even supposed to listen to it unless it is confirmed with evidence by two or three witnesses. It continues, "As for those who are guilty and persist in sin, rebuke and admonish them in the presence of all, so that the rest may be warned and stand in wholesome awe and fear" (v. 20). The guy who continues to talk harshly about your pastor needs to be rebuked. You need to tell him to stop.

I found interesting wording of the same passage, 1 Timothy 5:17–20, in *The Message:*

> Give a bonus to leaders who do a good job, especially the ones who work hard at preaching and teaching. Scripture tells us, "Don't muzzle a working ox," and, "A worker deserves his pay." Don't listen to a complaint against a leader that isn't backed up by two or three responsible witnesses. If anyone falls into sin, call that person on the carpet. Those who are inclined that way will know right off they can't get by with it.

I like the part that says, "Two or three responsible witnesses." Not a person who doesn't have a clue about what is going on. And if anyone falls into sin, call that person on the carpet. I like that.

I believe that if you call someone out when he does something out of order, then others will definitely know that they need not try to get away with doing the same thing—especially when it comes to bad-mouthing your pastor. When they open their mouths to say he is taking money from the church, don't sit there and consider the validity of the statement even for one second. When you know the procedure for handling money within your particular church, you don't have to sit there and listen to that mess.

Read 1 Timothy 5:17 (TLB): "Pastors who do their work well should be paid well and should be highly appreciated, especially those who work hard at both preaching and teaching." For some reason, people think that preachers don't work, but I can speak from personal experience. Before we built the World Dome, I would get up at 4:00 A.M. every Sunday to preach the 6:00 A.M., 7:30 A.M., 10:00 A.M., and 12:30 P.M. services, and I did that for almost two years. Often, I would leave the fourth service and fly across country to preach somewhere else. I'm not complaining because that's what God has called me to do, but I'll have to tell you it's hard work.

When I go out of town, people ask me to bring them back a T-shirt from whatever city or country I'm traveling to, as if I'm going on vacation. I've got a calling and an anointing on my life to do certain things, and I must do what I'm supposed to do. I'm not going on vacation, as some folks are led to believe. I know that a lot of preachers would not have preached four services, but I'm so hungry to see people delivered out of darkness that I'll preach as many times a day as necessary.

People need to know when their pastor lines up with what's taught in 1 Timothy 5:17. If your minister is hardworking and preaches and teaches the Word of God and does his job well, he should be compensated for it. Understand that those of us charged with doing God's work are accomplishing the very things God has ordained us to accomplish.

Not long ago, a man from Brazil was praying and asking God what he could do for his country. He wanted to know who could minister to the people of Brazil. God told him to get up from prayer and turn on the television. There I was preaching in Jacksonville, Florida, and this man heard me. God told him that I was one of those chosen to minister to his countrymen. He sent us a broadcast contract to cover the entire South American continent, including Argentina, Peru, and Brazil. The broadcast will be translated into whatever languages are needed to reach those people.

Things like that don't just happen. Work is required to do those broadcasts. We're also covering the entire United Kingdom, Puerto Rico, Nigeria, parts of South Africa, and even Australia! We're making a mark that cannot be erased.

I don't feed my church members spiritual baby food. I feed them well from the meat of God's Word. I spend time with God so that they can live the life of prosperity that the Lord has called them to live. Whether or not folks agree with the idea of prosperity will not stop me or my congregation from prospering. I will not rob this church, and that's exactly what I would be doing if I gave in to my detractors and stopped preaching the Word on prosperity.

The anointing brings about sweatless victory. For that reason, people actually believe that I don't work hard at preaching and teaching. When I was preaching those four services, I'd be so tired that I was dizzy the next morning when I got up. There were times when I thought I'd actually pass out in the pulpit from exhaustion. According to researchers in the medical field, preaching one hour is comparable to exerting eight hours of energy on other jobs. So, for all intents and purposes, I was expending thirty-two hours of energy just by preaching. It certainly wasn't money that moved me to preach like that.

During the course of a year, I probably preach more than five hundred sermons and travel to eighty or more places to preach. It's not unusual for me to preach at home, leave the pulpit, and fly to another country to do the same thing all over again. I do what I do because I've been called by God. I have a charge to keep and God to glorify. If this description gives you a better understanding of what a pastor goes through, it's worth it to me to tell you our church business.

Our system of checks and balances assures that nothing can happen in our ministry without more than one person knowing about it. Someone else has been appointed to know what I know about financial matters in the church.

Don't listen to complaints against the pastor unless there are two or three seasoned and responsible witnesses to accuse him. If he has really sinned, then he should be rebuked in front of the whole church so that no one else will follow his example.

I want to take you to a few more Scriptures on this. If you're not convinced in this area, you'll continue to fall back into the same trap, and it will continue to hinder your blessings. Take a look at 1 Corinthians 9:7–14:

> Who goeth a warfare any time at his own charges? who planteth a vineyard, and eateth not of the fruit thereof? or who feedeth a flock, and eateth not of the milk of the flock?

Say I these things as a man? or saith not the law the same also? For it is written in the law of Moses, Thou shalt not muzzle the mouth of the ox that treadeth out the corn. Doth God take care for oxen? Or saith he it altogether for our sakes? For our sakes, no doubt, this is written: that he that ploweth should plow in hope; and that he that thresheth in hope should be partaker of his hope. If we have sown unto you spiritual things, is it a great thing if we shall reap your carnal things? If others be partakers of this power over you, are not we rather? Nevertheless we have not used this power; but suffer all things, lest we should hinder the gospel of Christ. Do ye not know that they which minister about holy things live of the things of the temple? and they which wait at the altar are partakers with the altar? Even so hath the Lord ordained that they which preach the gospel should live of the gospel.

That same passage in *The Living Bible* reads,

What soldier in the army has to pay his own expenses? And have you ever heard of a farmer who harvests his crop and doesn't have the right to eat some of it? What shepherd takes care of a flock of sheep and goats and isn't allowed to drink some of the milk? And I'm not merely quoting the opinions of men as to what is right. I'm telling you what God's law says. For in the law God gave to Moses he said that you must not put a muzzle on an ox to keep it from eating when it is treading out the wheat. Do you suppose God was thinking only about oxen when he said this? Wasn't he also thinking about us? Of course he was. He said this to show us that Christian workers should be paid by those they help. Those who do the plowing and threshing should expect some share of the harvest. We have planted good spiritual seed in your souls. Is it too much to ask, in return, for mere food and clothing? You give them to others who preach to you, and you should. But shouldn't we have an even greater right to them? Yet we have never used this right, but supply our own needs without your help. We have never demanded payment of any kind for fear that, if we did, you might be less interested in our message to you from Christ. Don't you realize that God told those working in his temple to take for their own needs some of the food brought there as gifts to him? And those who work at the altar of God get a share of the food that is brought by those offering it to the Lord. In the same way the Lord has given orders that those who preach the Gospel should be supported by those who accept it.

You know, of course, that since you have read Scripture on this subject, people will be coming out of the woodwork saying ugly things about your pastor. The Bible says that the thief comes to steal, kill, and destroy, so he will try to take away the Word you've just read (John 10:10).

The Amplified Bible says,

[Consider this:] What soldier at any time serves at his own expense? Who plants a vineyard and does not eat any of the fruit of it? Who tends a flock and does not partake of the milk of the flock? Do I say this only on human authority and as a man reasons? Does not the Law endorse the same principle? For in the Law of Moses it is written, You shall not muzzle an ox when it is treading out the corn. Is it [only] for oxen that God cares? Or does He speak certainly and entirely for our sakes? [Assuredly] it is written for our sakes, because the plowman ought to plow in hope, and the thresher ought to thresh in expectation of partaking of the harvest. If we have sown [the seed of]spiritual good among you, [is it too] much if we reap from your material benefits? If others share in this rightful claim upon you, do not we [have a still better and greater claim]? However, we have never exercised this right, but we endure everything rather than put a hindrance in the way [of the spread] of the good news (the Gospel) of Christ. Do you not know that those men who are employed in the services of the temple get their food from the temple? And that those who tend the altar share with the altar [in the offerings brought]? (On the same principle) the Lord directed that those who publish the good news (the Gospel) should live (get their maintenance) by the Gospel. (1 Cor. 9:7–14)

Friend, it's absolutely clear to me that people who make their living by teaching and preaching the good news about Jesus, the Anointed One, are supposed to prosper in every area of their lives and ministries. When they do, don't look down on them. Sow seed into their lives to bring about your prosperity. Repeatedly, the Scriptures warn against muzzling an ox. Churches today do that by refusing to adequately take care of their men of God, so therefore they close their mouths.

Make a decision not to allow doubt and unbelief where your pastor is concerned to hinder what God wants to do in your life. If you don't trust your pastor, leave that church. It makes no sense to stay in a church where you don't have confidence in the man leading the flock. Go to a church where you can believe the one ministering to you because to do otherwise is to put your life on the line. It's a trick of the devil when people say things against your pastor. Don't allow yourself to take in those things, and let them know that they can't get away with saying those things to you. Put yourself in a position for your prosperity to be manifested.

CHAPTER 13

STEP 12:
DILIGENTLY SEEK AND PRACTICE
THE PRESENCE OF GOD

꙰

By now you know that this book is not dealing only with money; it also discusses control of circumstances—yours and someone else's. A friend of mine said that the best revenge in the world is success. When you can succeed in the things of God and turn around and walk in love to be a blessing to a person who has mistreated you, that is the ultimate in prosperous living. As I mentioned earlier, it's not complete prosperity when you're the only one affected by it. It doesn't reach its peak until you can affect someone else's life.

There has been some resistance around the country against those of us who are preaching prosperity because many think it relates only to money. It makes a difference when you understand what this message is truly about. It is not just about money. What good is money when you're dying of cancer? What good is money when you're on your fifth marriage, and it's about to end in divorce as the previous four have?

This twelfth step requires you to do a lot of self-evaluation. If I'm stepping on your toes during this chapter, don't despair. I promise you that if you'll read it through to the end and make up your mind to practice what this step teaches, you will never be the same again.

I don't know how you define Christianity. Maybe you define it as wearing a title, having a position, being a member of a church, or singing in the choir. I define it as being hooked up with God. To me, it's learning all you can learn about Him and allowing Him to change you so that you conform to His image. If you rely on the definition of titles, it won't be long before you run into someone who has the title, but no evidence of being a Christian. There is something about an individual who spends time in the presence of God. Nothing else can compare to time spent with the Father.

People often ask me how they can hear from God. There is only one way to achieve a heart that is receptive to hearing His Word, and that is to spend time with Him. I'm sure that many Christians want to spend time with Him, but wanting to do it and doing it are two different things. People want the anointing, blessings, wisdom, and voice of God in their lives, but they may not be willing to commit and invest the time necessary in His presence to achieve these things.

It's amazing how many people go to church on Sunday without taking time when they woke up to pray and seek God's face. Folks figure that since they're going to church anyway, why waste the time (as if spending time with Him could ever be considered a waste)?

My purpose in this chapter is for you to get a revelation of what happens when you spend quality time in the presence of the Lord. I want to convince you, through the Word of God, to stir yourself up and rededicate yourself to seeking God. The answers you are looking for can be found only in God and with God, but you'll never know until you take the initiative to go where He is.

How do you think I cope with my dilemmas? Do you think that I call my spiritual father, Kenneth Copeland, every time I have a problem? Most of the time I can't even locate him because he is so busy traveling the world evangelizing. I get in the presence of God and stay there until He speaks to my heart and tells me what I need to do to get out of that situation. Stop trying to put people in the place of spending this necessary, quality time with God. People are not your way out; God is.

Your healing is in the presence of God. The answers about how to get along with your mate, raise your children, buy a house, and handle your boss are all found in Him. When you get to heaven, you'll find out that these answers were available to you all the time, but you never took the time to get what God had already reserved for you.

You try to use the counsel of men and think that it will do more for you than a talk with the Lord. Why? Because getting in His presence is going to cost you something. It will cost time, effort, and overcoming the feeling of not wanting to pray or talk to God at a particular time. You might not actually say out loud that you don't want to talk with Him, but that's what it all boils down to. Who says you have to talk? Maybe part of your problem is that you talk too much. Sometimes getting away from everything and everybody, lying down in the presence of God, and letting Him talk to you would make a difference.

God said, "If My people who are called by My name will humble themselves, and pray and seek My face, and turn from their wicked ways, then I will hear from heaven, and will forgive their sin and heal their land" (2 Chron. 7:14 NKJV). That's a word from on high, and it will work for anyone. Instead of letting the preacher do all the praying, it's vital for you to do what is necessary to have God operating fully in your life.

You need to do everything you can to get before the Lord. I want you to make up your mind that you will never miss another day of having daily contact with God. You can't be anointed if you're not spending time with God. You can't become wise if you're not spending time with God. He wants to inhabit your praise. He wants to let you know that He is there for you, but you must have contact with Him.

Some of us spend more time with the devil in negative meditation than we do in the meditation of God's Word. When you worry, that's what you're doing—meditating on the things of the devil. Worry brings about fear of what's going to happen, and as you well know, God has not given you the spirit of fear (2 Tim. 1:7).

You can put a lot of effort into thinking about your problems and everything that's going on in your life, and the entire time God is trying to get your attention. Meanwhile, He is trying to get you to where He is so that He can show you the way out of no way. He is just waiting for you to show up. If you'll come out of your comfort zone and stop doing the least you can do for God, you'll see a change. You should want to be everything God has called you to be, no matter what it takes for that to happen.

You need to acquire a hunger and a thirst for God. Then instead of going into prayer because you *have to,* you go into prayer because you earnestly *want to.* God has dealt with me about that. I used to pray for the anointing to be upon my life. He let me know that He didn't want me to come to Him because

I had figured out a way to stay anointed. He wanted me to come to Him just because I wanted to be with Him.

If you're sick, I want you to know that you don't have to be sick anymore. If you're depressed, hurt, lonely, or sad, Jesus is here to remove those burdens and destroy those yokes. He is anointed to do just that. Instead of waiting to see if He will show up, learn how to go into His presence to obtain the things you want and need. You've already been given the go-ahead in His Word to "come boldly to the throne of grace, that [you] may obtain mercy and find grace to help in time of need" (Heb. 4:16 NKJV).

It's time for you to stop sitting back and waiting to see if God is going to show up: "He sought God in the days of Zechariah, who had understanding in the visions of God: and as long as he sought the LORD, God made him to prosper" (2 Chron. 26:5). Isn't it interesting that when Christians are in trouble, they, too, often run from God instead of running to Him? As long as you seek the Lord, God will cause you to prosper. When you can't figure it out and don't know the difference between your left and your right, don't stop seeking God.

When you don't have a clue about why a certain thing happened or when your best friend does you wrong, don't stop seeking God. When a family member dies or when you lose your job, don't stop seeking God. You've come too far to stop now, and I guarantee that He is not going to stop seeking you.

Something wonderful happens in the life of the believer who continues to seek God regardless of the situations in life, good or bad. Sometimes, life can be so good that you'll stop seeking God because you think you've made it. When times were bad, you sought Him night and day. You wouldn't miss a morning of praying and reading your Bible. As a matter of fact, you took your Bible everywhere you went, and you even had a bunch of colored markers to highlight your Scriptures. But as soon as God delivered you from the desert you were traveling across, you forgot about the One who gave you the power to reach your destination. I'm telling you, as long as you seek God, He will prosper you—He promised: "Without faith it is impossible to please him: for he that cometh to God must believe that he is, and that he is a rewarder of them that diligently seek him" (Heb. 11:6). He will reward those who have turned seeking Him into a way of life.

I seek God because I am in love with Him. I'm not always after what's in His hands. I'm not always after what He can give me or how He can bless me. Remember, blessings are no good unless they can extend beyond you to someone else. God's objective is to bless all the families of the earth. You are blessed by God to be a blessing to someone else. There is no reason for you to be blessed if you are unable or unwilling to fulfill the other side of the equation and be a blessing to others.

As I said, I'm not always after what's in His hands. I want to know what makes Him tick. When I read a sweet verse about being thought of as the apple of His eye (Zech. 2:8), I knew then that He considers us to be something special. He created you and me for the purpose of fellowship and praise, and most of us don't spend time with Him at all.

God is asking for the equivalent of a daily phone call home. If you're guilty of this level of neglect of the Father, let me warn you that you'll reap what you sow. This is a simple message, but if you ever get it, it will change your entire life. God is saying, "I will surely reward the man who will seek Me."

Did you know that it's possible for your prosperity to increase if you increase the amount of time spent in His presence? God has committed Himself to you, and now it's time for you to commit yourself to Him: "Behold, I am with thee, and will keep thee in all places whither thou goest, and will bring thee again into this land; for I will not leave thee, until I have done that which I have spoken to thee of" (Gen. 28:15).

That's an awesome promise to stand on. I've been on commercial airplanes and heard talk about crashing. The first thing that comes to my mind is that God will not leave me until He has brought to pass what He promised. He is committed to you. He is committed to me. He even says that He will never leave us or forsake us, and He will be with us until the end of the world (Heb. 13:5; Matt. 28:20).

If it doesn't seem that He is there for you, maybe you never show up. He is ready to do exceedingly abundantly above all that you can ask or think, but you never show up (Eph. 3:20).

He can't even talk with you because you're too busy. He tries to warn you about becoming involved in certain things, but you can't hear Him. Your heart has hardened, and it is not nearly as pliable as it was when you first were born again. If that's not the case, you've gotten so spiritually deep that you talk all the time in prayer and He can't get a word in edgewise.

I heard this story about a man who had five days in which he needed to hear from God. On the first day, he went into prayer and started talking in tongues the whole time. The second day, he spoke in tongues. The third day, it was getting closer to the deadline, so he was talking in tongues really fast. The fourth day, he went into prayer and started speaking in tongues and became so choked up that he couldn't say anything. God said, "It's about time you were quiet. Now I can tell you what you need to hear."

God is always talking, always transmitting, but He often can't get through to you, the receiver: "Thus saith the LORD that created thee, O Jacob, and he that formed thee, O Israel, Fear not: for I have redeemed thee, I have called thee by thy name; thou art mine" (Isa. 43:1). He is committed: "When thou passest through the waters, I will be with thee; and through the rivers, they shall not overflow thee: when thou walkest through the fire, thou shalt not be burned; neither shall the flame kindle upon thee. For I am the Lord thy God, the Holy One of Israel, thy Savior" (Isa. 43:2–3).

You must change your picture of God. He is not a big judge sitting on the throne ready to throw a lightning bolt at you when you mess up. God is filled with mercy and tender loving-kindness for you. God wants you to succeed more than you want to succeed. He is ready to do everything for you that you'll let Him do. He wants to overtake you with blessings. By making you aware of His presence, He wants to let you know that He has everything you need or desire.

He is definitely not against you, as some Christians would have you believe. He is not the One making people addicted to drugs. Some people foolishly say that God brings sickness to teach us a lesson. God does not have to use the devices of the devil to try to show us something. People actually believe that He causes car wrecks and kills folks because they aren't living right. Either they're mistaken, or the Bible is wrong. And we all know that the Word is truth. God is not a killer. The devil comes to steal, kill, and destroy (John 10:10).

On the other hand, God sent Jesus to give us life more abundantly. We need to learn who our Father really is. He is not the One giving cancer to folks or putting AIDS on the earth to prove anything to homosexuals. God is in love with all people. He hates the sin, but He loves the people. He is pulling for people to come out of their sin, so they can be cleansed by the blood of Jesus. He is intent on your coming to Him in prayer and fellowship. His hands are tied if you have sin in your life.

Do you know why God can't release His full blessings upon you when you have sin in your life? He is not punishing you. On the contrary, He is being merciful. God can have only one response to sin, and that is to wipe it out. Sin, in the presence of God, makes His presence destructive. He is not telling you to get the sin out of your life because He wants to see how good a Christian you can be. He wants the sin out of your life because He wants to come into your life and bless you. However, He can't abide in the same space as the sin.

All this time you've managed to turn God into the bad guy, as if He is trying to wreck your life. He asks that you take care of the temple of your body so that He can dwell within you to lead and guide you. Even if you don't love God, He has set His will to love you.

As for the notion that God stops loving you when you mess up, forget it because it's not so. God has His hands on you, and when you do something ridiculous and take two steps away from righteousness, He is not the One who moved; you are. He never moves, and the door will always be left wide open so that whenever you decide to come back, you can pick up where you left off.

God is not interested in taking you back to the land of Egypt where you were going through hardship and suffering. That's not His style. His aim is to pick you up and move you on to the destiny He has designed for you to reach in His glory: "He said, My presence shall go with thee, and I will give thee rest" (Ex. 33:14).

Whenever you are trying to figure out things and succeed based solely on your education, you are always going to struggle. But God is telling you that if you will come into His presence, you'll find the rest there you need. Where your education didn't work for you quite the way you had hoped, God will give you the wisdom to do what your education didn't show you. He is letting you know that if you come to Him, He'll give you a marketing plan they didn't reveal to you in business school, and He'll teach you things the world could never have prepared you for. In His presence is the secret of how to be healed and stay healed in your body, even if the medication you need is not yet available in the natural world.

You never have to go to bed worried about your problem because in God there is a way out. He'll show you how to prosper in the marriage that everyone said was going to fail and end in divorce—if you come into His presence. What disturbs you disturbs your heavenly Father. All He asks is that you stop pushing Him out of your life and thinking about Him only on Sunday morning. He wants to be involved in every aspect of your life— the good, the bad, and the ugly. God wants in. He wants to make the good better, improve the bad, and give you rest and peace from the ugly side of life.

Moses had such a revelation of the necessity of God's presence, he responded by saying, "If thy presence go not with me, carry us not up hence" (Ex. 33:15). He was talking about the promised land. As good as he knew it would be there, he didn't want to go there without God. That should be your attitude. Wherever God is not, you shouldn't want to be, either. When you feel that way, there is no debate about whether or not it's right to go nightclubbing on the weekend. Just ask yourself, Is God going to be there?

Ask the same question regarding churches. When someone asks, "Do you want to go to my church?" find out first if the Lord will be present and accounted for.

In His presence, child of God, is rest. It's time for you to cease struggling. It's time for you to cease trying to figure out something God has already perfected. You don't need to worry about something God has already fixed.

I have proclaimed to my congregation that this is the year of the fix. Whatever in your life has been broken, torn apart, damaged, or destroyed, God is going to fix it. This is the time of great restoration, and God is in the restoring business: "I will restore to you the years that the locust hath eaten, the cankerworm, and the caterpillar, and the palmerworm, my great army which I sent among you. And ye shall eat in plenty, and be satisfied, and praise the name of the LORD your God, that hath dealt wondrously with you: and my people shall never be ashamed" (Joel 2:25–26).

Being a part of your life means so much to God. You need to take time out to thank Him for who He is and for what He has done in your life. During the day, stop and thank Him for the many blessings He has bestowed upon you by saying,

> Father, I worship You, and glorify Your name. I worship You, Lord, and apologize for being insensitive to how much You want to love me and spend time with me. I didn't know, God. I just didn't know. But now that I do know, You are more than welcome in my life. Forgive me for turning what should be a relationship with You into a religion. It's a personal relationship, and I know that now. It's a relationship, and not something I do on Sundays, but every minute of every day of the life You have blessed me to live. I give You praise, Lord, and thank You in advance for everything You will do in my life today and for every day to come. I thank You for my healing, my deliverance, my provision, and my peace. In Jesus' name, Amen.

Shout unto God with a voice of triumph and a mouth filled with praise. Praise Him now for the prosperity He has promised in His Word.

Don't forget what the Bible says about Joseph: "The LORD was with Joseph" (Gen. 39:2). The following verses say that folks could look at Joseph and see that the Lord was by his side. Your prosperity, therefore, is going to be based on your relationship and time spent with the Lord, and it will be obvious to all.

We read about Enoch in the book of Genesis: "Enoch lived sixty and five years, and begat Methuselah: and Enoch walked with God after he begat Methuselah three hundred years, and begat sons and daughters" (Gen. 5:21–22). I used to read that but didn't get excited until I realized what that truly meant. Enoch was in the presence of God: "And all the days of Enoch were three hundred sixty and five years" (Gen. 5:23).

That's living, isn't it? He was probably still acting like a teenager at age one hundred: "And Enoch walked with God: and he was not; for God took him" (Gen. 5:24). Back up a minute. Do you see the significance of that last statement? The fellowship was so great, God enjoyed Enoch so much, that one day God took him on home with Him.

One day—and it won't be very long—the Bible says, "Behold, I show you a mystery; we shall not all sleep, but we shall all be changed, in a moment, in the twinkling of an eye, at the last trump" (1 Cor. 15:51–52). God is going to take us out of here! Can you imagine a time of fellowship so awesome that God takes you on home to be with Him? Enoch never saw death. In fact, he has been hanging out with God all this time.

Can you imagine the things he is learning? In view of all that, how can you say you have a personal relationship with Jesus when you hardly ever give Him your personal time? I'm not talking about going to church on Sunday so that you can sing your solo. I'm talking about making a quality decision to spend at least one hour a day in fellowship with God. You have twenty-four hours available to you. Can't you devote at least one of them to God?

Jesus took His disciples into the Garden of Gethsemane and told them that He was going to pray, that He wanted them to watch, be alert, and wait for Him to return. You know the rest of the story: "And he cometh unto the disciples, and findeth them asleep, and saith unto Peter, What, could ye not watch with me one hour? Watch and pray, that ye enter not into temptation: the spirit indeed is willing, but the flesh is weak" (Matt. 26:40–41).

Jesus wanted to know why they couldn't find it in themselves to give up one hour of their time, especially after all He had personally been through with them. And what happened? Perhaps they wanted to. Maybe their spirits were willing, but you know that old flesh. They didn't understand that the one hour in the morning with God is designed to defeat their weak flesh.

Every time you spend an hour with God, you're overcoming your flesh and setting yourself up for the remainder of the day to overcome anything that will try to attack your flesh. Staying in the presence of God for one hour, just you and God, is not too much to ask.

As soon as you can get away from false teaching about prayer, you'll be all right. The theory that prayer is a monologue could not be farther from the truth. Prayer is a dialogue between you and God. What makes you think that it's necessary for you to do all the talking?

Have you ever heard God say to you, "I love you"? If you have, I know you will never be the same. Well, if He can say that, don't you know that He has much more to say to you?

The book of Proverbs is full of wisdom for us: "Trust in the LORD with all thine heart; and lean not unto thine own understanding. In all thy ways acknowledge him, and he shall direct thy paths" (Prov. 3:5–6). God wants to direct your paths. He wants to direct your living and your giving. He is just waiting for you to show up, not as a superstar Christian, but as you are. Even if your life is messed up, He says, "Come to Me, and I'll straighten everything out." But because the world has convinced you that your time could be much better spent than "wasting" it on God, you won't do as He asks. People have tried to convince you that you can use your time doing something else besides lying on your face on the floor and talking to a God you can't see.

I'll tell you this, and then I'll confirm it with Scripture. Nothing in the world, or in the world system, can replace time spent in the presence of God. Nothing compares to fellowship with Him.

In the book of Acts, a group of intelligent men encountered two of the disciples, whose actions they could not attribute to their education: "Now when they saw the boldness of Peter and John, and perceived that they were unlearned and ignorant men, they marveled; and they took knowledge of them, that they had been with Jesus" (Acts 4:13).

How would you like to be in a business meeting where everyone except you had a master's degree, but you were the only one to come up with the answer the group was looking for? Your time spent in the presence of God will cause people to wonder. They'll want to know why you have the peace that passes all understanding, while they're concerned about getting laid off. That's when you let them know that God has already assured you in His Word that no matter what happens, all of your needs will be met according to His riches in glory through and by Christ Jesus (Phil. 4:19).

People pass their time worrying when they don't have the knowledge of God and His Word. Why waste time worrying when you can spend that time putting faith pressure on getting things to happen to change your present condition? God is knocking, but no one will come to the door. Psalm 16:11 tells you that in His presence is fullness of joy. Nehemiah 8:10 tells you that the joy of the Lord is your strength. You will find strength in the presence of the Lord.

When trouble comes, a lot of folks will run to everything the world has invented to get out of that trouble. They will run everywhere but to God simply because they don't see His presence as being the place to find their answer. Their mistake is not seeing how being with God can help their situation.

I pray that the information contained within these pages will turn your life around and make you want to change for the better. You should be tired of a contemporary gospel message that doesn't require you to change. The attitude of most people is that you can preach to me if you don't wrinkle my clothes or offend me in some way. Well, I'm not that type of sugar-coated preacher. I can't do that. If you're going to hell, I've got to tell you that you're going to hell. And believe me, I won't lose any sleep over it. But I will lose sleep if I tell you that you're all right.

I must be the freest person on the face of the earth. It doesn't bother me anymore what people say about me. It used to, but it doesn't now.

Why should you be concerned about what someone says about you? Is he paying for your utilities or putting food on your table? It's truly a waste of time. And when someone walks up to you to gossip about a brother or sister in Christ, tell him that you don't want to hear it. Let him know that you have better things to do than to hear what people are saying about you or about someone else. That comes under the heading of corrupt communication, and the Bible warns about that (Eph. 4:29).

You must realize that not everyone is your friend. There is a difference between friendship and association. You may have many associates, but friendship demands covenant commitment. Your spouse is your friend. Your children are your friends. If there is no commitment and no covenant, don't call people friends; call them associates. You've had association with them in the past. They came to your outer court, but you wouldn't let them into your inner court, and they definitely couldn't get into your Holy of Holies. Christians spend more time in the presence of "he said, she said," than in the presence of God.

I'm tired of playing these religious, church games. If you want God, God wants you. Get it together and let's go on and get to heaven and do what we've got to do. Stop playing around. If you're going to do this thing, do it right. Stop listening to rumors and gossip about you. Learn how to love yourself. If no one is saying things to you that you like to hear, talk to yourself. Encourage yourself.

Read this about Jehoshaphat: "It came to pass after this also, that the children of Moab, and the children of Ammon, and with them other beside the Ammonites, came against Jehoshaphat to battle" (2 Chron. 20:1). A great number of people were coming against Jehoshaphat to battle. Something like all those demons of hell trying to come against some of you in battle. Have you been there before?

Look at how Jehoshaphat handled the dilemma: "Jehoshaphat feared, and set himself to seek the LORD" (2 Chron.

20:3). What was the solution? He decided to talk with the Lord, to seek God. The old boy figured it was a tough one. Time to seek God. He had everyone on the east coast trying to come against him. Jehoshaphat decided it was a job for the Almighty, so he "proclaimed a fast" (2 Chron. 20:3).

He needed to make sure that nothing was clogging up his receiving mechanism, so he called a fast. Don't misunderstand. Fasting does not impress God. Fasting is for your benefit. You may be praying, but you may need to go on a fast to clean out your receiver so that heaven can transmit to you and you'll be able to hear.

You don't have to go on a forty-day fast, either. Some people fast for twenty days and then brag about it. They end up looking skinny, and that will be their only benefit (Matt. 6:16–18). Usually, I'll fast a day, get what I need, and then eat something. God is not impressed with my hunger pangs.

The most important reward that comes from fasting is that you can receive what you need to hear from on high. That's it. Fasting, however, has become a lost art in some of the faith churches. Remember, faith comes by hearing. But if you can't hear, then what? Fasting cleans the wax out of your spiritual ears.

Jehoshaphat sought the Lord and proclaimed a fast throughout all of Judah. He brought everyone in on it. If the situation will affect the entire family, include them in the fast. Let everyone get in on it:

> Judah gathered themselves together, to ask help of the LORD:
> even out of all the cities of Judah they came to seek the LORD.
> And Jehoshaphat stood in the congregation of Judah and
> Jerusalem, in the house of the LORD, before the new court,

and said, O LORD God of our fathers, art not thou God in heaven? (2 Chron. 20:4–6)

Pay careful attention to how he was seeking God. He was in God's presence, but he was not begging and pleading and crying, "Oh, help me, Lord, please." No, he said,

> Art not thou God in heaven? and rulest not thou over all the kingdoms of the heathen? and in thine hand is there not power and might, so that none is able to withstand thee? Art not thou our God, who didst drive out the inhabitants of this land before thy people Israel, and gavest it to the seed of Abraham thy friend for ever? (2 Chron. 20:6–7)

Are You not the God who will supply all of my needs according to His riches in glory? Are You not the God who can give me what I need to pay this unexpected bill? Are You not the God who can give my husband a job? Are You not the God who saved me, sanctified me, filled me with the Holy Spirit, and gave me favor? What Jehoshaphat did, and what you must do when you pray, was to declare the covenant agreement with God:

> They dwelt therein, and have built thee a sanctuary therein for thy name, saying, If, when evil cometh upon us, as the sword, judgment, or pestilence, or famine, we stand before this house, and in thy presence, (for thy name is in this house,) and cry unto thee in our affliction, then thou wilt hear and help. (2 Chron. 20:8–9)

He said, "In the time of trouble, I'm standing in the presence of the Lord, and I'm going to cry out before You. You will hear me, and You will help me." That was a covenant man talking. He didn't go to God begging and pleading, flailing his arms and crying, "Oh, please, Lord, help me." When you do that, you are demonstrating that you're a stranger to your covenant.

A man who knows his God, his covenant, and the promises of God does not have to go begging and bawling. He goes right up before his covenant partner and says, "God, according to Your Word, which You promised in blood, You will hear me, and You will help me. You said that by the stripes of Jesus, I am healed. I didn't mention anything about healing. You brought it up. You said that You were going to meet my needs according to Your riches in glory. I didn't say it. You did. You even said that You were going to bless me on my way in and on my way out, and that I would be the head and not the tail. You said I would be above, and never, ever again beneath. You said to put You in remembrance of Your Word, so I'm reminding You of what You said about this situation (Isa. 43:26).

"You said You'd take sickness and disease from my midst (Ex. 23:25). You said that my enemies will come against me one way and flee seven ways (Deut. 28:7). I'm not so smart that I would say these things without having heard them from You. You said it, God, and I know now that You will help."

You see, that's the way covenant people talk. They say what God has already said in His Word. They don't go into prayer crying and pleading and acting like people in the world. They don't tell God what the world said about them failing, or that the doctor says they're about to die. No, God doesn't want to hear all that mess. He didn't say those things. He wants a covenant person to come before Him and declare the covenant.

That's what being born again is all about. Pleading your case before God. Going to Him and saying, "Lord, I'm guilty of all the charges. I was doomed, damned, and disgraced, but Jesus with His precious love saved me by His grace. He dropped the charges and dismissed my case, and now I stand cleansed by the blood of Jesus. I have wronged no man. I am innocent, I am now born again, and I plead my case based on what You said and what You've done."

Stop begging God and sounding like an unbeliever. Some people have the nerve to go before God and tell Him if He doesn't act in a certain way, by a specific time, they're going to die. You're right—you will die if you continue to speak such negative things. When you go into prayer, continue to remind Him of His Word. This may sound arrogant, but you have the right to say to God, "If You didn't mean what You said in Your Word, You shouldn't have said it." But, the Bible says, God cannot lie. If He said it, He will do it, and if He spoke it, He will bring it to pass (Isa. 46:11).

Just make sure that you know what He said and that you say what He said. If you stay home looking at reruns of *Gunsmoke* instead of going to church to hear what "thus saith the Lord," you'll never know what to pray.

During our church services, if I discern in my spirit that someone is having a problem with the message I'm teaching, I tell him to wait in the car. Since you're reading and not in one of my services, I'll tell you to put the book down and chew on what I've just said. Get your concordance, find these verses in your Bible, and then let's continue. I know that this is different from the teaching you hear in some traditional churches, but it's good and it's God. You'll be all right.

God will hear, and He will help:

Now, behold, the children of Ammon and Moab and mount Seir, whom thou wouldest not let Israel invade, when they came out of the land of Egypt, but they turned from them, and destroyed them not; behold, I say, how they reward us, to come to cast us out of thy possession, which thou hast given us to inherit. O our God, wilt thou not judge them? for we have no might against this great company that cometh against us. (2 Chron. 20:10–12)

You may have been like that: "Dear God, all that's coming against me, and I haven't got enough to fight it."

I'm sure that you have been in a situation where you didn't know which way to turn. Look toward God for an answer. Take your eyes off your problem and put them on God: "Neither know we what to do: but our eyes are upon thee" (2 Chron. 20:12).

God is in the midst: "And all Judah stood before the LORD, with their little ones, their wives, and their children. Then upon Jahaziel the son of Zechariah, the son of Benaiah, the son of Jeiel, the son of Mattaniah, a Levite of the sons of Asaph, came the Spirit of the LORD in the midst of the congregation" (2 Chron. 20:13–14). Isn't it something how He shows up when you talk covenant talk?

Read farther in the story: "He said, Hearken ye, all Judah, and ye inhabitants of Jerusalem, and thou king Jehoshaphat, thus saith the LORD unto you, Be not afraid nor dismayed by reason of this great multitude; for the battle is not yours, but God's" (2 Chron. 20:15). The Spirit of God showed up, and He said, "Step aside, little covenant partner. I hear what you've been saying, and I see what you've been going through. Now your Big Covenant Partner is here. Step aside and take a seat. Let Me wrap this thing up and do what's got to be done."

He told them to do these things tomorrow: "Tomorrow go ye

down against them: behold, they come up by the cliff" (2 Chron. 20:16); and "Ye shall not need to fight" (2 Chron. 20:17). When God says to do something tomorrow, don't take it upon yourself to do it today because He has designated the anointing to be there for a specific time. Some of you are fighting when you don't need to.

I took a group of our church teenagers on an outing, and they ended up wanting to fight with a restaurant manager who tried to take their money by overcharging them. They called me to tell me what was going on, and I told them they didn't have to fight. I dealt with the manager and then followed up on what I said to him at a later date.

By the time things settled down, I explained to the boys that when God is your God, you don't need to use your fists because the Lord will fight your battles for you. I congratulated the boys for holding their tempers, for holding up a standard of manhood and not acting like thugs. You're not a man because you use your fists. Using your fists means that you weren't smart enough to figure out any other way to settle the situation.

How many battles have you fought when you didn't have to? How many fights have you gotten into when you could have held your peace?

> Set yourselves, stand ye still, and see the salvation of the LORD with you, O Judah and Jerusalem: fear not, nor be dismayed; tomorrow go out against them: for the LORD will be with you. And Jehoshaphat bowed his head with his face to the ground: and all Judah and the inhabitants of Jerusalem fell before the LORD, worshiping the LORD. And the Levites, of the children of the Kohathites, and of the children of the Korhites, stood up to praise the LORD. (2 Chron. 20:17–19)

Look at that. Right in the middle of trouble they praised the Lord. How did they do it? The Bible says "with a loud voice on high" (2 Chron. 20:19). They didn't praise the Lord in a whisper because they didn't want to be embarrassed. You know what I mean. They didn't talk softly because they were ashamed to let people know they were thankful to God for what He had done. No, the Bible says they praised Him with a loud voice.

I believe you need to use a loud voice in the middle of your trouble when you can't figure out how to get out of where you are. You need to open up your mouth and say, "Hallelujah!" You need to open up your mouth and shout unto God with a voice of triumph. Watch how many heads turn when you yell "Jesus" in a public place.

> They rose early in the morning, and went forth into the wilderness of Tekoa: and as they went forth, Jehoshaphat stood and said, Hear me, O Judah, and ye inhabitants of Jerusalem; Believe in the LORD your God, so shall ye be established; believe his prophets, so shall ye prosper. And when he had consulted with the people, he appointed singers unto the LORD, and that should praise the beauty of holiness, as they went out before the army, and to say, Praise the LORD; for his mercy endureth for ever. (2 Chron. 20:20–21)

Armies had gathered to destroy them, yet Jehoshaphat didn't think to get their army together. He didn't call the military. He called the praisers and the singers and told them to go right up to the line of the opposing forces and say, "Praise the Lord." You need to understand what God was getting them to do. He promised in His Word to occupy the praise of His people. He shows up when you praise Him.

Picture this. God is hanging around in heaven, and He hears someone down on earth saying, "Praise the Lord." He says, "Uh-oh, wait a minute, y'all. Gotta go. Enoch, I'll see you when I get back. Somebody's praising, and I promised that when My people praise Me, I will inhabit their praise. I told them that I'd be in the midst of them. I will occupy their presence with My presence."

If you can get God to show up where your trouble is, your trouble will have to go. No army in the world is more powerful than the presence of the Lord when He shows up: "When they began to sing and to praise, the LORD set ambushments against the children of Ammon, Moab, and mount Seir, which were come against Judah; and they were smitten" (2 Chron. 20:22).

They had a praise service right in the middle of the battlefield. They got right up in the faces of their opponents and sang, "This is the day that the Lord has made. Hit me, man. I will rejoice. Go ahead and hit me if you can—and be glad in it. This is the day that the Lord has made. I will rejoice. It's pretty hard to hit a dancing, praising target, but you're welcome to try. Be glad in it." They were praising and dancing and shouting "Hallelujah!" all over the place.

In the meantime, the opposing army was baffled. The soldiers didn't know what to make of folks praising the Lord while they were being attacked: "For the children of Ammon and Moab stood up against the inhabitants of mount Seir, utterly to slay and destroy them: and when they had made an end of the inhabitants of Seir, every one helped to destroy another" (2 Chron. 20:23).

The opposing army killed itself off. How? Well, you know those boys on the opposing side, they were no doubt engaged in conversations like these:

"Throw your spear."

"I can't. My mama said not to ever disrupt a man when he's praising the Lord."

"Sergeant?"

"Yes, sir?"

"I command you to throw your spear."

"No, sir. I can't do it."

"Sergeant, if you don't throw your spear at them, I'll throw my spear at you."

Well, behind the commanding officer was the sergeant's cousin.

"You'd better not hurt my cousin. My mama told me that family have to protect one another. If you touch my cousin, I'll have to touch you."

And behind the sergeant's cousin was the commander's cousin.

"You'd better not touch my cousin."

And then his cousin and another's cousin got involved, and before you know it, God had the thing set up where they started fighting one another. And while they were killing one another over here, on the other side, they continued to sing, "This is the day that the Lord has made." While they were praising the Lord, the presence of God settled in. He started moving in on the other side. They couldn't see Him. They couldn't feel Him. They couldn't touch Him, but He was moving in the midst of the enemy.

Continue with this passage with me to see how complete God is. He can do better than any military force in this country or the world:

When Judah came toward the watch tower in the wilderness, they looked unto the multitude, and, behold, they were dead bodies fallen to the earth, and none escaped. And when Jehoshaphat and his people came to take away the spoil of them, they found among them in abundance both riches with the dead bodies, and precious jewels, which they stripped off for themselves, more than they could carry away: and they were three days in gathering. (2 Chron. 20:24–25)

Everything that was lost in preparation for the battle was restored. They didn't have to fight; they just went to God. After He was finished, there was so much booty left over from the battle that it took them three full days to gather it up.

Friend, you've tried the rest, now try the best. Stop turning to the world's system for a solution to your problems, and come to God. Seek Him. Seek His presence. In His presence is everything you need. You're never wasting your time when you're in the presence of God. Prayer is time wisely and well spent. I challenge you from this point on, no matter what happens, to seek God's presence. It will change your life. If you can't hear from Him, go on a fast and repent of your sins. Cleanse yourself from your wicked ways. Draw nigh to Him, and He will draw nigh to you.

CHAPTER 14

STEP 13:
QUICKLY REPENT
WHEN NECESSARY

〰〰

Let's talk about sin. Having an accurate picture of our God is important to this discussion. Someone, somewhere, somehow has deceived us into thinking that God is looking forward to our messing up.

We've been led to believe that He has a lightning bolt ready to zap us when we sin. That's not our God. He is ready to forgive you. He is ready to cleanse you from all unrighteousness. He does not want to see you fail. He wants to provide every possible way for you to get to heaven and for you to have abundant life here on earth.

Repentance for sin is vital. That is Step 13. The way you deal with this area will be another barometer for your level of prosperity. You must deal with sin, or it will deal with you.

Check out 2 Chronicles 24:20: "The Spirit of God came upon Zechariah the son of Jehoida the priest, which stood above the people, and said unto them, Thus saith God, Why transgress ye the commandments of the LORD, that ye cannot prosper?" When you transgress the commandments of God, the Bible says that you cannot prosper. Your prosperity is going to be blocked if you don't deal with your transgression. You can't take the sin, stick it in a box, and pretend that it doesn't exist—especially when the blood of Jesus has been given to us. The blood of Jesus works when you're dirty. Just as the purpose of soap is to clean your body when you're dirty, the blood of Jesus works when you need to be cleansed of sin.

What good is it to have the blood of Jesus and not take advantage of it when you need it? Transgression will stop your prosperity: "Because ye have forsaken the LORD, he hath also forsaken you" (2 Chron. 24:20).

You can tithe, plant, give, and sow, but if you don't deal with the sin in your life and repent, it will prevent you from prospering. Saved people don't like to talk about sin because they've gotten so used to programs and twelve steps to recovery. But, folks, this is something that has to be dealt with. It's time to get the sin out of the camp, so it's necessary to understand what repentance is, and then go ahead and do it.

The word *repent* literally means "to change your mind, your heart, and your position." In effect, you're making a 180-degree turn, and instead of facing the problem, you've turned your back on it. You don't want to make a 360-degree turn because you'll end up right where you started—in sin. It's not just a matter of being sorry. It's a matter of turning completely away from your transgression.

The person who will continue to do what he does in the booth, in the back corner in the dark, will never prosper: "He that covereth his sins shall not prosper: but whoso confesseth and forsaketh them shall have mercy" (Prov. 28:13). No one ever knows he is sinning because he knows all the right Christian moves. He knows how to lift his hands and wave just right. He knows exactly what to say and how to smile when he comes to church.

Now, let me say this to you, and I want you to mark this in your life forever. The sin in your life that you fail to deal with will ultimately be responsible for your downfall. Sin won't be your downfall. The sin that you fail to deal with will get you each and every time. It's the stuff that you keep shoving in that big box because you don't know who to talk to about it.

I know that some Christians have put up an unrealistic display of what it means to be in Christ. Some people act as if we're flawless, and that's not true.

And then there are those "holier than thou" types who are down on people who make mistakes. When folks mess up, they want to run from the church because they think that the rest of us are too perfect for them to try and live up to our standards. Everyone can have a look of perfection in church on Sunday mornings, but the real person is evident at home. Somehow, some way, we need to begin to convey the reality of Christian life—the good part and the bad.

You don't need to pretend that you didn't have struggles in the past. You can really minister to someone who is going through the things you've gone through and let him know that God will work it out. Have you ever in your Christian life felt as if you were the only one going through a certain trial? You thought that because someone was a Christian, surely he couldn't be going through anything too tough. But the reality was that he did; he just didn't tell you about it. I can't say that I blame him because we have to be careful about telling our business to others.

Don't become upset if you tell your personal business to someone you shouldn't have, and he tells someone else. When you told that person, you knew good and well that he was not allowed to enter into the Holiest of Holies, that sacred place reserved for the people with whom you share covenant and commitment. He was in the outer court, but you shared an inner court issue with him and he spread your business. It's your fault when things like that happen because you allow yourself to have expectations of people with whom there is no commitment. You know you're not supposed to tell someone you're only vaguely familiar with such personal things about yourself. Then when your expectation that he was going to protect you is not fulfilled, your disappointment is unreasonable.

It amazes me how Christians put on such a display of holiness, as if there were never any problems in their lives. Not that you should go around and blab your business, as I said earlier, but you've gone through some trials that would make a great testimony in the proper place and time. Your experiences can be used to deliver someone else. When God delivered you, He didn't do it just for you; He did it for someone else. He never delivers you only for your benefit. He delivers you so that your testimony can minister to someone else. That can't happen if you're walking around in this pretense of being flawless.

To balance all of this, hear me out. I'm not saying that you should walk around talking about the negative things of your past. I'm saying that when the opportunity presents itself, you should be willing to share the other side of Christianity so that people won't get a false picture of it. Folks need to know that getting from where they are to where God wants them to be is part of the package and they're not going through something strange. The Bible says that you're not going through something uncommon to man:

There hath no temptation [trial, test, problem] taken you but such as is common to man: but God is faithful, who will not suffer you to be tempted above that ye are able [to hear]; but will with the temptation [trial, test, problem] also make a way to escape, that ye may be able to bear [up under] it. (1 Cor. 10:13)

When I run into folks who haven't been to church in a while and I ask them why, they often admit that they slid back into drugs, pornography, or the things that they were trying to get out of. I tell them that's no reason to leave God. When you get into trouble, don't run *from* God; run *to* Him. In our church, we have a ministry for alcoholics, drug addicts, and people who want to overcome homosexuality. Most of the time these people want to come back to church, but "something always comes up" to prevent them.

When they fall back into sin, they feel as if they can't come to church because everyone there is perfect. If the people who are going through the trials would understand that there are other Christians struggling with drug, alcohol, and sex problems who come to church and press their way to deliverance, it would give them hope. They would learn that they don't have to leave the church because there are others like them who kept coming and eventually were delivered from their problem.

When someone confides information concerning an addiction or problem, don't criticize him by saying, "You haven't prayed enough," or "Maybe your giving is the problem." That may be true, but that's not how you handle a situation when someone comes to you hurting and in trouble. You need to get on a person's level before you can bring him up to where he is supposed to be. I'm not suggesting that you compromise. Before

Jesus could bring us up to the kingdom of God, He had to come down to earth; He had to come down to our level. I'm talking about the level of sin. The Bible says He was made sin that we might be made the righteousness of God (2 Cor. 5:21).

You will never bring people up to the necessary level by acting as if you are flawless. You know the truth of the matter: you're not perfect, just forgiven.

You have an Advocate with the Father, and the blood of Jesus cleanses you from all your sins. It's not over because you sin or because you missed God. You may fall down 100 times; make up your mind to get up 101 times.

Make up your mind that you're never going to quit because God will never quit on you. He is not going to throw you away. He is not the type of God who says, "I don't want to have anything to do with you because you messed up." God is used to us messing up. He is our Father, and He knows how to deal with us. That is why He gave us Jesus. God is ever ready to take care of our sin.

Don't run away from your church because you've messed up. God is trying to get you to your destiny. God's attitude toward sin is this: "Go and get yourself clean, and let's pick up where you left off."

What would you do if you fell into a mud puddle? You'd go home and take a bath, right? You're not going to sit in the puddle and cry about being dirty. So, when you sin, take a shower in God's forgiveness. God is trying to tell you that He needs for you to get to some place. But what do you say? "I'm not worthy." God knew that when He came to save you. Jesus is worthy, and God sees you only through the righteous blood of Jesus. He sees you as being cleansed from head to toe.

You must get ahold of this thing, or you'll continue to give the devil this weapon to use against you. He knows that if he can get most of us to sin just one time, it will stop us for a month. It will stop you from praying, going to church, and getting the Word. If he can get you into the habit of not getting the Word, he can get you to quit. And if he can get you to quit, he can kill you. The wages of sin is death (Rom. 6:23). He wants to bring you into hell and move you out of his way—all because you didn't understand the concept of repentance.

"He that covereth his sins shall not prosper" (Prov. 28:13). You don't have to cover up your sins. Instead, confess your sins to God. The first Scripture I learned when I was born again was 1 John 1:9. It says, "If we confess our sins, he is faithful and just to forgive us our sins, and to cleanse us from all unrighteousness."

Proverbs 28:13 also says that if you confess and forsake your sins, God will show you mercy. The process is not over when you confess. When you do that, God is ready to do His part, but your part is to forsake the sin. God takes your sin and throws it as far away as the east is from the west, and you know they'll never touch. Your sin lands in the Sea of Forgetfulness, and He remembers it no more. If you came back to God five minutes after you confessed that sin and asked Him if He remembered the sin you just talked to Him about, He would say, "No, I forgot." He'll check your record and let you know that it's not written down anywhere in His books. Glory to God!

But the forsaking part is your job. That's when you truly get to repentance. You have to leave the sin, turn your back on it, and keep going toward God. Now, you may shake while you're walking away from it, but keep walking and you'll be fine. You might be going through withdrawal symptoms, but keep on keeping on. Make up your mind that you will not turn toward that sin anymore. Once you forsake it, you can't be playing around with it.

Do you understand what I'm trying to tell you? If you're a single man and you go out on a date with a single woman, you get her home, and she has one of those remote control fireplaces, don't tell yourself that you can handle the situation. Many have failed the test before you. Don't stay around telling yourself that you're strong because you're not strong enough to handle the temptation alone. Once the music comes on and it's a song that used to be your favorite when you were in the world, you'll start to break down.

When you're leaving drugs, you can't hang around with people who are still using them. It's the same with alcohol. There is no such thing as a casual drink for someone who has been delivered from alcoholism. You've already turned your back on the sin. Don't get involved again. You might not want to hear this, but turning your back on your sin may require you to turn your back on a particular person or relationship. Maybe not forever, but you know what's best for you in this instance.

You need to disconnect from the person that you find yourself gossiping with, smoking with, or doing whatever you're trying to get away from. Then build yourself up in the Lord, strong, powerful, and ready to go. At that time God may call you back to minister to the person, but you must use wisdom. The Bible says that "evil communications corrupt good manners" (1 Cor. 15:33).

You must learn whom and what you can hang around. Anyone you associate with becomes a part of you, so you have to be discerning enough to know who and what is healthy for you. You must recognize which people and situations put you in a position to turn back to that sin. And when you figure that out, figure out a way to stay away from it.

I'm not for one minute suggesting that you turn your back on the sinner. No, don't fellowship with the sinner. You can have a relationship where you're giving the Word, encouragement, and spiritual support to that person, but don't put yourself in a receiving mode with a person like that. If that person is consumed by drugs and you're full of the Holy Spirit, there can be no fellowship: "For what fellowship hath righteousness with unrighteousness? and what communion hath light with darkness?" (2 Cor. 6:14).

According to the Bible, there can be no impartation in that relationship. But don't get a "holier than thou" attitude where you feel as if you can't touch someone made unclean by sin. Someone had to touch your sin at some point for you to come to salvation. Don't forget that. All I'm saying is that this relationship has to be guarded. You must be disciplined enough that his corruption doesn't rub off on you, but instead your holiness rubs off on him.

I believe that if you need repentance, before you finish reading this book, you will have gone to the throne of mercy to be washed in the blood. God's mercy will replace any sin in which you may be involved.

Read Ezekiel 18:30: "Therefore I will judge you, O house of Israel, every one according to his ways, saith the Lord GOD. Repent, and turn yourselves from all your transgressions; so iniquity shall not be your ruin." There can be no true repentance unless you turn yourself away from sin. Repentance is a form of sanctification. You separate from sin, but you turn to righteousness. Sin—any sin—will ruin you.

God is not telling you to repent of your sins because He is a mean Father. He says this because He doesn't want you to be ruined: "Cast away from you all your transgressions, whereby ye have transgressed; and make you a new heart and a new spirit: for why will ye die, O house of Israel? For I have no pleasure in the death of him that dieth, saith the Lord GOD: wherefore turn yourselves, and live ye" (Ezek. 18:31–32).

Just what is He saying? He is telling you that sin will kill you and that He doesn't take any pleasure in seeing you killed by your sin. Remember that God created this whole system based on the method of seedtime and harvest. If a man sows sin, the law of the harvest says that he will harvest death. If a man sows obedience, the law of the harvest says that he will harvest an eternal, abundant God-kind of life.

Sin will definitely kill you. For example, you can't keep committing adultery and expect to live a long time. If the offended spouse doesn't kill you first, disease will. You can't continue to have sexual activity outside of marriage. You can go around bragging about how many people you've been intimate with, but statistics dictate that someone is liable to send you home with more than you bargained for. Things have gotten to the point that sin is magnified, and the results of your sin are magnified because the devil wants you dead. It takes only one experience for sin to produce death.

The word *death* literally means "separation." When a man sins, just as Adam did in the Garden of Eden, it separates him from the presence of God. The problem with that, of course, is that everything you need is found in the presence of God: answers, healing, prosperity. But sin separates you from all that. Ultimately, it will separate your spirit and soul from your body because that's what sin does—it kills. That's why God doesn't want you involved in it. You may think that God is trying to spoil the party, but remember this: God is in love with you, and He knows the results of sin.

One day you are going to be able to recognize that and start seeing things God's way. God is not about ruining your life or spoiling your fun. He wants to do just the opposite: "Because he considereth, and turneth away from all his transgressions that he hath committed, he shall surely live" (Ezek. 18:28).

Sin by itself won't kill you. When you won't turn away from it, it finally gets you. The solution to sin is to repent, to turn away from it completely. As long as you're repenting of it and forsaking your sin, it can't kill you. Just as the man in this verse turned away and lived, so will you if you walk away from your transgressions.

Maybe you haven't done anything wrong that you would consider a "real" sin, but there is such a thing as a sin of omission as well as a sin of commission. When you don't do what God wants you to do or what you know you're supposed to do, that's a sin of omission. You've sinned because you haven't done something. If I were to stop preaching (I've thought about it at least five hundred times), that for me would be a sin of omission.

A couple of times I thought since I was doing so much traveling, I could let the pastor thing go. I figured I would travel, go home, and not have to deal with a flock. God soon straightened out my thinking. He told me that if I left the pastorate, I would also leave the anointing under which I operate because He called me to be a pastor first and foremost. The evangelist office that I operate in is in addition to the office of pastor. God let me know that I was not to leave my primary calling and function only in the role of an evangelist.

If God told you to join the music ministry, but you won't because someone in the choir offended you, you're out of order. You need to get where God has called you to be because God doesn't change His mind about what He has called you to do (Rom. 11:29). It amazes me how some Christians make it seem that God is always changing His mind: "Well, the Lord told me to do this, but now He told me to do that."

It seems to me that you don't know what the Lord told you to do. One day you're in the children's ministry, then you try your hand in the outreach ministry, and the next thing you know, you've started a ministry to the poor. Get the sin out of your life so that you can hear clearly what the Lord would have you do: "For the wages of sin is death; but the gift of God is eternal life through Jesus Christ our Lord" (Rom. 6:23).

If you operate in sin, it will cause a separation between you and the God-kind of life, the abundant life. He wants you to turn away from sin and toward something of His choosing. What is it? "Repent ye: for the kingdom of heaven is at hand" (Matt. 3:2).

The Message puts it in these terms: "Change your life. God's kingdom is here." The way God does things is at hand. Turn away from your old way of doing things, and turn toward God's way of doing things. The world has seduced some of us. We find ourselves doing what the world does, the way the world does things, and being concerned about what the world is concerned about. We call right what the world calls right, and we call wrong what the world calls wrong. God says it's time to change your mind, your heart, and your direction because there is a better way of doing things. The kingdom of God is here.

Turn away from the world's way, and turn to Him because He has another way for you to live. It's time to repent, folks.

There were present at that season some that told him of the Galileans, whose blood Pilate had mingled with their sacrifices. And Jesus answering said unto them, Suppose ye that these Galileans were sinners above all the Galileans, because they suffered such things? I tell you, Nay: but, except ye repent, ye shall all likewise perish. (Luke 13:1–3)

It's not His will that you perish, but He says except you repent, you will. Those of you who are reading this and still living your wild, crazy lifestyle have this opportunity to get a word of repentance. It's the same message John the Baptist preached as he cried out loud in the wilderness, "Repent for the remission of your sins!" Don't allow yourself to be seduced by the world.

Hear what God is saying. Don't perish in your sins: "Repent ye therefore, and be converted, that your sins may be blotted out" (Acts 3:19). Isn't that something? God says He'll blot out your sins—just like you take a bottle of white liquid from the office supply store and blot out your typing mistakes and make them disappear. When you repent at the end of this chapter, God will blot out everything that has happened before today. Afterward, you can say, "I'm innocent; I'm innocent."

That God can erase your sins is a wonderful thing. But if God has blotted out your sins, why do you keep bringing them up? You know what the devil is going to do? He is going to give you a one-hundred-inch screen picture of what you did last week or last night. When the devil starts talking to you, plead the blood.

Remember that policeman during the O. J. Simpson trial? Every time they asked him a question, he pleaded the Fifth Amendment. No matter what they asked him, he said, "I plead the Fifth." Likewise, when the devil shows up on your doorstep and says, "Now you know good and well you don't feel like tithing," don't sit there and argue; just say, "I plead the blood."

"You know you have no business waving your hands in praise service as if you're flawless."

"I plead the blood."

"After what you did two weeks ago, do you actually think all you have to do is to confess your sin and turn away from it? How many times have you already turned away from it? My last count seems to be close to one hundred times. Do you actually think God is forgiving you as many times as you've repented and gone back to that same sin?"

Don't sit there and argue with him. Just say, "I plead the blood."

What does it mean to plead the blood? It means to remind the devil of what the blood has bought for you. Tell him that by the blood of Jesus, you have the blood-bought right to cry, "Abba Father." Not because you're flawless, but because of the blood, your sins are forgiven. It's not a question of whether you deserve it. The fact is that almighty God has given His blood, and by that blood, you have the right to all God has to offer.

If you buy into the lies of the devil, you'll believe that you don't have the right to healing because you're not perfect. He'll tell you that because you sinned, you're going to die, and you'll believe him. That's another opportunity to plead the blood Jesus shed at Calvary over any situation that Satan might try to present to you. Tell him that in the name of Jesus, you have the right to the same healing power made available to all anointed men and women of God.

Some of us won't receive prosperity because we think we don't have a right to it. Too many Christians think that because of past sins, they don't have a right. They say, "Why would God want to do something for me?"—not realizing that God wants to bless them. God wants to prove His love to you. He wants to let you know that you're not the old, good-for-nothing sinner you've been convinced that you are. Contrary to what you may have heard, you're still His child. And from now until the end of the world, He will continue to welcome you back into the fold once you've repented. God won't give up on you.

Maybe you are in a backslidden position, but God is married to the backslider (Jer. 3:14). Not only that, He honors the covenant between you and Him. Leave that sin. Kick that habit. Do away with that addiction. Tell Jesus that you're coming back to Him. Ask Him to cleanse you and wash you so that you can begin afresh, white as snow.

Look at what happens when you repent: "Repent ye therefore, and be converted, that your sins may be blotted out, when the times of refreshing shall come from the presence of the Lord" (Acts 3:19). The times of refreshing come. From where? From the presence of the Lord. He wants you to repent so that you can receive the refreshment found only in Him. For some of you carrying around a heavy load from your transgressions, carrying around condemnation and guilt, this is the time for your refreshing. You've been letting the devil counsel, accuse, and condemn you for too long. The moment you repent, God will quickly rush in like a Father who has missed His child. He has missed the fellowship with you: "As many as I love, I rebuke" (Rev. 3:19). A rebuke is an act of love. Someone corrects you because he loves you. Otherwise, it wouldn't matter to him what you did.

Read farther: "As many as I love, I rebuke and chasten: be zealous therefore, and repent. Behold, I stand at the door" (Rev. 3:19–20). Man, that blesses me. Here God is telling you to repent because He is knocking on the door of your heart. He wants to come in and be in covenant with you, but He is waiting on you to change your direction. You see, many things of God await you. Your prosperity, your control of every situation in life is there, waiting for you to repent of some things. You can't ignore the sin in your life. You must deal with it, stop letting it hinder your blessings, and move on to the wonderful things of God.

Have you ever met someone who tries to take every word the preacher says and use it as a license to sin? You know the type. He says, "Yeah, well all I know is that Jesus turned water into wine, so drinking must be all right."

True Christians, those who love God and want to keep His commandments, are not looking for a way to sin. They're looking for a way out of sin.

Stop looking for a way out of righteousness. Oftentimes if you need to ask someone about what you're doing, it's wrong.

"Now, Pastor, I have a question. Is it wrong to . . . ?"

"You don't even have to finish. It's wrong for you to . . ."

"How do you know? I haven't even asked the question!"

"First of all, you're asking me, and second, you're convicted by it."

Don't despair. Jesus is there waiting on you to change your plans. Here's a verse that gives you a reason to repent: "Therefore thou art inexcusable, O man, whosoever thou art that judgest: for wherein thou judgest another, thou condemnest thyself" (Rom. 2:1). So, be careful how you talk about someone else's problems. You may not be going through what he is going through, but you will if you keep opening your mouth. Let's stop throwing people away when we see them messing up and stop judging them to others. Go to them personally and tell them, in love, they need to repent.

Someone says, "Child, I'm not gossiping, but you need to know this so that you can pray for so-and-so." That's just a religious excuse for you to let corrupt communication come out of your mouth. That's just an excuse for you to gossip. When someone starts off the conversation like that, ask him if he has gone to the sister or brother in question to discuss it with that person first. Tell him you're sure the person would appreciate hearing about it firsthand. Let him know that if he had brought it up when it happened the last time, the person might not have had another occasion to fall into the same sin.

Don't say you love someone when you're not willing to talk to him about something you've seen him do wrong. If the church would do that, it would eliminate many problems. We pass things by as if we don't see them because we don't want to rock the boat. Sometimes you must have a rocky boat before you can have smooth sailing.

Don't judge one another. Otherwise you'll end up condemning yourself. Whatever you do is based on the law of seedtime and harvest. Nowadays the church as a whole chooses to believe the worst of people. Never mind what she said or he said; choose to believe the best.

Christians have the biggest gossip parties. Have you ever talked about someone and agreed with the ugly things being said, only to meet that person and find out he is nothing like you were told? Doesn't that make you feel guilty? You can't even look him straight in the eye knowing how you've wronged him behind his back. You're embarrassed because you opened yourself up to believe a lie. Don't judge anyone else; judge yourself. You have enough work to do in that area.

God judges you according to truth: "We are sure that the judgment of God is according to truth against them which commit such things. And thinkest thou this, O man, that judgest them which do such things, and doest the same, that thou shalt escape the judgment of God?" (Rom. 2:2–3). When you're constantly being judged by others, they're probably in the back, in the corner, or in the dark doing the same things they're judging you for. Don't worry because their sin will also find them out.

The goodness of God will lead you to repent: "Or despisest thou the riches of his goodness and forbearance and longsuffering; not knowing that the goodness of God leadeth thee to repentance?" (Rom. 2:4). Every time I've repented in my life, the goodness of God motivated me to do so. Some of you reading this book have gotten involved in some things in your past that could have killed you. When you think about the goodness of God, you know good and well that you're still here because of Him.

You know how many times you've messed up and how many times He has forgiven you. He keeps restoring you, meeting your needs, and healing your body even though you know you didn't deserve all that kindness. That type of treatment from a loving God would lead anyone to repent. Even before you were formed into a thought, Jesus died for you.

You don't have to share your business with anyone, but you and God know that you should have ended up with a disease as often as you allowed your body to be used outside marriage. And you used to drive drunk all the time; it's only the goodness of God that kept you from wrecking your car and your life. Those drugs you used to take could have gone past stringing you out. They could have strung you up like a noose around your neck, but God brought you out of what should have happened to a place where you can give Him praise and thanksgiving.

Don't you ever forget about the goodness that He has shown in your life. He woke you up this morning and started you on your way. When you think of the goodness of the Lord and what He has done for you, your soul ought to shout "Hallelujah!" because He has given you the victory.

After that, it's easy to convince yourself not to stay in that sin any longer. You can't quit on God because He'll never quit on you. You can't turn your back on Him because He didn't turn His back on you. You must get your life right. Doing that may be rough, but you must get it right. Why? Because God has been too good to you.

God changed you from the inside out. He gave you a new name, a new walk, and a new talk. He has even changed the way you think. He has given you His name, His anointing, His Spirit, His Word, and His presence. He has given you all that heaven has to offer and everything that pertains to life and godliness (2 Peter 1:3).

He gave you healing when your body was sick, comforted you when you were lonely, and lifted you up when you thought you were going to be defeated. He has brought you from a mighty long way. Don't let one day of sin keep you from the presence of God. He fed you when you were hungry, remember. You didn't know where the food was coming from, but God showed up just in time. Repent, and keep going.

Do you realize how hard it was for Jesus to die on that cross? Yet He did it. And you can die to yourself, put some things to death in your life, and turn things around. It's not over. Despite what you've been led to believe, the devil has not defeated you. The Word of God has given you an upper hand over the devil. You see, he forgot about the anointing. He forgot that as a child of the King, you have the burden-removing, yoke-destroying power of God operating in your life.

The mercy of God will replace your sin, and His goodness will move you to repentance. If you think that it doesn't do you any good to repent, stop those thoughts right now. I don't care if you've repented of the same sin for what seems like a thousand times. Do whatever it takes for you to see Jesus. Don't talk yourself into hell. Think about God's goodness and how you don't want to leave Him. You need to settle things right now by saying, "Lord, I don't care what happens. I'm never going to leave You. I don't care what comes. I'm never going to leave You."

You may have strayed, but God is waiting to welcome you back. Keep getting up when you fall, and press your way toward what God has in store for you. You have enough Word in you to overcome whatever is trying to bring you down. Don't let condemnation or guilt keep you away: "There is therefore now no condemnation to those who are in Christ Jesus" (Rom. 8:1 NKJV).

Walking in the spirit of life in Christ Jesus will make you free from the law of sin and death. Walk in His Word. Receive by faith the forgiveness of God. Once you ask for forgiveness, it will be given: "Now I rejoice, not that ye were made sorry, but that ye sorrowed to repentance: for ye were made sorry after a godly manner, that ye might receive damage by us in nothing" (2 Cor. 7:9).

It's one thing to be sorry for something; it's another thing altogether to repent. Most people are sorry when they get caught in their sin, but that doesn't necessarily mean they've repented. When you catch little Johnny, he is sorry he got caught with his hand in the cookie jar, but that doesn't keep him from doing it again.

I like David, in spite of all the things he did. David was a murderer. He sent a man to his death because he had slept with the man's wife and gotten her pregnant. But you know what I like about David? When he was pressed down with a broken heart and a contrite spirit, he repented before God. Now he leads the testimony that says David is a man after God's own heart because he did the will of the Father (Acts 13:22).

It's not over because you missed the mark. Just repent. This entire chapter is a call for repentance, a call for you to come out of sin.

God wants us all to come to repentance: "The Lord is not slack concerning his promise, as some men count slackness; but is longsuffering to us-ward, not willing that any should perish, but that all should come to repentance" (2 Peter 3:9).

Before you go on to the final chapter of this book, say this prayer of confession out loud:

Father, I pray in Jesus' name for an anointing in my life to remove every burden and destroy every yoke. I ask now that You wash me white as snow. I call upon the blood of Jesus to wash away every sin so that I will not walk in condemnation and I will be free to take hold of what is rightfully mine by the blood of Jesus.

I thank You, Father God, that through the blood of Jesus, I have a right to receive forgiveness of all my sins. I thank You that by the blood of Jesus, and because I have made the decision to confess my sins and forsake them, I will prosper. I declare right now that the time of repentance is at hand. I will turn from the things that separate me from God and from prosperity. I repent of all sin in Jesus' name. I declare that I am forgiven. I am innocent. I have wronged no man. My sins have been blotted out, and I thank You, Lord, that I will not be condemned by the sins of my past. Jesus has washed my past away, and I am free from the things that are behind me.

If you're not saved, you need to be born again to avail yourself of the things of God. When He makes promises in His Word, the promises are for His own. If you don't know for sure whether or not you're saved, don't take a chance on your salvation. Turn to Appendix A, and pray the prayer that will get you saved.

You've tried the rest. Now try the best. If you need to rededicate your life to Christ, now is the time to do that. Come back into the light after experimenting with darkness. As I mentioned earlier in this chapter, God is married to the backslider. He doesn't want to share you with the world, so take time out to officially come back to God.

As you will learn in the upcoming chapter, a heavenly prayer language is essential. I don't know what you've heard about tongues in the past, but in the next chapter I will show you how praying in tongues affects your prosperity.

Last, but not least, some people reading this book have put off the decision to join a church. God has not called you to visit churches until Jesus returns. He told Elijah to go to a certain brook, and there He would sustain him (1 Kings 17:3–4).

Find the brook to which God is calling you to be fed the meat of His Word. Hook up with a church that teaches and preaches the Word of God in a way that you can understand and in a way that your life will be changed for the better as a result.

This is indeed a time of refreshing. Take full advantage of this opportunity to come to Jesus.

CHAPTER 15

STEP 14:
LEARN HOW TO INTERCEDE

～～

Last, but in no way to be considered least, the final step toward prosperity is intercession. All of the steps are important, but this is a vital step without which prosperity can't take place. Intercession is a key that will allow you to operate in the blessing of having total control in all areas of your life. I have found through Scripture and my personal experience that what you make happen in someone else's life is what God is going to cause to happen in your life. When you can get the attention off your needs, your hurt, and your pain and focus it on someone else, God is able to take care of you.

My hurts, my pains, and my disappointments should not be important to me, but they should be important to you. Your hurts, your pains, and your disappointments should not be important to you, but they should be important to someone else.

In this step, you will learn how to take the attention you've been giving yourself and direct it toward someone else. In this way, you will get your needs met while you intercede in prayer for the needs of someone else. The Bible tells us,

> Pray for the peace of Jerusalem: they shall prosper that love thee. Peace be within thy walls, and prosperity within thy palaces. (Ps. 122:6–7)

> I have set watchmen upon thy walls, O Jerusalem, which shall never hold their peace day nor night: ye that make mention of the LORD, keep not silence. (Isa. 62:6)

The praying mentioned in the psalm is considered intercession. In Isaiah, the watchmen upon the walls are intercessors. The Word tells us that if we pray for the peace of Jerusalem, the Lord will cause us to prosper. When I first got revelation of this Scripture, I thought, *Well, there must be a number of people who pray for Jerusalem every day.* Then again, probably a greater number of people don't even think about Jerusalem. But since the Bible talks about prospering folks who take time to send up prayers for that nation, I figured I would go ahead and start mentioning Jerusalem in every one of my prayers.

I thought that there might be a little extra something God wanted to give me for praying for this city. I mean, I need to take every avenue of prosperity offered to me. If you visit our church, you'll hear that we pray for peace in Jerusalem during our corporate prayer time on Saturday morning and before each service.

While we pray for peace in that nation, we're maintaining peace in our own country. That's God's way of doing things. Whatever you want to happen in your life, extend it to someone else, and God will see that you get the benefit for interceding.

We read Luke 22:32: "But I have prayed for thee, that thy

faith fail not." If you look up this verse in your Bible, the words will probably be in red. Why? Because they are Jesus' words. As you can see, Jesus' faith never failed because He was praying that our faith would not fail. Let's continue reading in that passage: "And when thou art converted."

Do you see that? Oh, I know what to do when I am saved. When you are converted, once you've been born again, here's what the Lord wants you to do: "Strengthen thy brethren."

You're now born again. You're now converted. What do you do? The Lord says that you are to strengthen the brethren. I can think of no more effective way to strengthen sisters and brothers in Christ than intercession. When I begin to intercede, I empower the brethren. When I pray for you, I strengthen you, and you don't even know it. Someone is praying for you, and you're being strengthened as a result of his prayers. Glory be to God!

Jesus is asking you to help your brother through prayer, the way He is helping you in Luke 22:32—through intercessory prayer. Intercessory prayer will enable prosperity to camp out on your doorstep because you're no longer centering your thoughts on yourself. You have directed your thinking and praying toward someone other than yourself.

Let's start with a basic foundation so that you can understand exactly what prayer is. It's more than talking to God. The way some people talk to God prevents Him from hearing anything they say, much less answer: "This is the confidence that we have in him, that, if we ask any thing according to his will, he heareth us" (1 John 5:14).

What is the will of God? The Word of God. The Word of God is the will of God, and the will of God is the Word of God. You've heard the old folks say, "Well, if'n it's the Lord's will." I submit to you that you will never know the Lord's will if you don't open the Word. His will is in His Word. His Word is His will.

According to this Scripture, He says this is how you can have confidence when you pray. I don't know about you, but there was a time in my life when I prayed and didn't have confidence that God heard my prayer. I didn't have confidence that He would even answer me. I was hoping that He would. Well, this Scripture gives me confidence.

If I ask according to His Word, then my guarantee is that He will hear me. But how can you ask according to His Word if you don't know His Word? Faith comes by hearing, and hearing by the Word of God. Faith can't come if you don't hear the Word. You can't change if you don't get the Word. So, what is the principal thing? The Word.

You are guaranteed that if you pray the Word, God will hear what you have to say. We have identified the Word as the prayer language. He has identified the Word as the language that operates the prayer system. You can beg and plead and cry all day long, but doing that will not cause God to hear you. Pray His Word, and you'll get His attention: "We know that he hear us" (1 John 5:15).

You know that He hears you because you've prayed His Word: "Whatsoever we ask, we know that we have the petitions that we desired of him" (1 John 5:15). How? Because you prayed His Word. Praying in this manner removes all doubt about whether or not your prayer reached the throne of God.

Prayer is a dialogue, which means that more than one person is involved. It is not a monologue, where you're the only one doing the talking. Traditionally, that's what we've been taught. We thought that if we spent a whole hour running our mouths

off to God, we were praying. But God doesn't get the opportunity to speak to us when we do that.

I did that one morning. I was running my mouth—just talking and looking at my watch. God asked me what I was doing.
You know what I was doing because you've probably done it
before many times. I was timing myself so that I could stop as
soon as I had spent my hour with God. I was about to turn my
intimate time with the Lord into a religion and a doctrine
because I read in Luke that Jesus said, "Could you not pray with
Me for one hour?"

I told God that I was looking at my watch to see how long I'd
been talking. He said, "Yes, I want you to see how long you've
been talking too."

He said, "Son, I'd like to talk to you during this time. I'd like
to impart wisdom into your life during this time. I'd like to say a
word to you that will make your day a whole lot easier. I'd like to
show you some things that are about to happen. Could I come in
and speak with you during this prayer time?"

Before then, I had never thought about giving God an opening in my prayer time to come in and speak with me. I was eager
to say yes to His question.

"Well, please be quiet and lie before me." So, I shut my
mouth. I could hardly stand it. Boy, the power of God came in,
and He began to speak things to me and give me answers to what
I had been praying about. When He finished, I started talking
again but was soon led to stop, so He could say something else to
me. That's prayer.

Not only that, but when you pray in that manner, you're sen-
sitizing your spirit to recognize the voice of God. When God tells
you not to go somewhere, you know His voice because you hear
it every day during your prayer time. Many people can't hear

from God because they don't practice hearing from God. They practice talking. That's a religious spirit. You feel as though you've accomplished something if you come out of the room hoarse and unable to speak above a whisper. That's what I used to do. But I've gotten much more from God by allowing prayer to be a two-way conversation rather than a speech during which my voice is the only one being heard.

Prayer is also saying to God what He has already said in His Word. He will talk to you in line with His Word, and the Word becomes the bridge that brings about communication. Prayer is a dialogue between you and God during which you say to God what He has already said in His Word.

For example, if you're praying to God for wisdom, the prayer would sound like this:

Father, I ask You for wisdom. According to Your Word, in the book of James, You said that if any man lacks wisdom, let him ask of God who will give to him liberally and upbraideth not. But let him ask in faith, and You said You'd do that. And I thank You for it right now. I know You hear me because I've prayed Your Word. You said in Your Word that if I pray according to Your Word and Your will, You will hear me. I've got confidence that You hear me as I pray, and I have what I've just asked for. So, I thank You, and I give You praise for it right now, in Jesus' name. Amen.

Then you pray until you're moved in your spirit to be quiet and listen to what God has to say. There's a tendency to believe that when you rise before daybreak to pray, you'll fall asleep if you stop talking. If you're in that position, do something about it. Who told you that you had to close your eyes when you pray? Where do we get all these silly traditions? Who told you to fold your hands when you pray?

We Christians love picking up little habits like these that the Bible hasn't said anything about. Get out of bed and walk if there is the possibility that you will fall asleep on God. He won't fall asleep on you. It says in Psalm 121 that He neither slumbers nor sleeps.

If you're a baby Christian, how are you going to pray with your eyes closed? I wish I had known this when I was a baby Christian. I was always running out of things to say because I didn't know any Scriptures. Then a dear brother said to me, "Open your eyes. What do you want to pray about? Get all the Scriptures lined up before you begin to pray." You may be saying, "But I can't feel anything then." Listen. You're not trying to *feel* anything. You're trying to get answers and to get some things to happen in your life.

That's what's wrong with us now. We're always wanting to feel something. You'll feel that debt after a while if you and God don't get together and figure out how to pay the bills. You're going to feel that sickness if you don't go to God and get answers on how to heal it. Jesus told His disciples to watch and pray. You need to open your eyes for that. You need to be alert.

After my brother in the Lord shared these things with me, I prayed about something from every page in the Bible that my eyes landed on. He tells us to put Him in remembrance of His Word, to declare of Him, and He will make demands on it for us. If you have a financial problem, find the promise where God said He would meet your need financially, and pray it to Him. Then say, "I know You heard me because I just read it out of the Book,

Lord." That's so simple. But, no, we want to teach people how to get all deep with this stuff. We've all been following bad tradition about how to pray.

Here is the proof of good prayer—evidence. The proof comes in what happens in your life after you pray.

We were in a meeting in Texas, and Brother Jesse Duplantis said something that thrilled me. He asked me if I was going to preach that night, and I told him that I was. He said, "Do you know what the devil hates to hear more than anything? He hates to hear the word *seed*. Every time he hears that word, he ducks his head out of the way."

You see, Genesis 3:15 says that the seed of the woman will bruise the devil's head. And every time he hears this, he ducks. Now what did you learn in one of the previous chapters? That God created the entire earth through seedtime and harvest.

If you don't have a prayer life, I encourage you to get one. Make time. No ifs, ands, or buts. Get your *but* out of the way, and make time to pray. It's vital for the Christian.

Now, what is intercessory prayer? Very simply put, intercession is prayer on behalf of another person. It's praying for others. Praying the Word, but praying it for others. Taking it a little deeper, intercessory prayer is an act of compassion and an act of mercy. Let me show you how.

Often, in the lives of people who are not operating according to God's method, not operating according to the law of seedtime and harvest, they find themselves reaping harvests that they did not sow. They are blessed when they know they did nothing to receive the blessings being manifested in their lives. They're protected when they know they should have died. Are you with me so far?

We know that everything on this planet operates by seedtime

and harvest. However, some people harvest things and can't figure out how the harvest happened. They weren't living right, but it came anyway.

Maybe that has happened to you. How can it be explained? Well, the mercy of God came upon your life, and the compassion of God came in and allowed you to get a harvest for which you didn't sow. How did you get it? An intercessor who sowed in your behalf gave birth to the harvest you're now reaping. It wasn't because of you; it was because of the intercessor who prayed for you. Do you know how you were born again? Someone had been praying for you and gave birth in the realm of the spirit, allowing God to bring that harvest to pass.

Isaiah 59:16 says, "And he saw that there was no man, and wondered that there was no intercessor." God sent Jesus so that He could begin to intercede. That was an act of mercy and compassion.

I'm glad to have intercession going on in my life, and you should be glad too. Because when you didn't deserve it, someone planted a seed for you.

Here's the deception. Some people will continue in the compromising lifestyle, thinking that it doesn't take all the stuff the pastor preaches about because they've gotten a harvest without doing all that stuff. Well, it wasn't because of what they were doing. With mercy and compassion, God can do whatever He wants to do. He is under obligation to those who are keeping His laws to harvest whatever they have sown. But that act of mercy and compassion shown through intercession has put many people in blessed positions that they would not otherwise have found themselves in. The intercession of the brethren strengthened them.

Intercession is not the responsibility only of the prayer

department. Intercession is something that God wants each and every one of us to get ahold of. Can you imagine what would happen if every Christian, on a daily basis, would pray for one hour for someone else besides himself? I'm telling you that the church would lack nothing.

Intercession is twofold. First, you can approach God in intercession for mercy and compassion on behalf of someone else. Second, you can come to God on behalf of an enemy coming against that person.

Let's say that John Brown is giving you a hard time at work. You come to work to do what you've been hired to do, and he behaves as if he is possessed by the devil. You'll find the key to this situation in the book of Ephesians: "Finally, my brethren, be strong in the Lord, and in the power of his might. Put on the whole armor of God, that ye may be able to stand against the wiles of the devil" (Eph. 6:10–11).

That old devil, you see, is trying to trick people. Paul was warning us to equip ourselves against those tricks: "For we wrestle not against flesh and blood" (Eph. 6:12). That means you're not wrestling against Mr. Brown who is against you. Your fight is not against flesh and blood, but against principalities, powers, rulers of the darkness of this world, and spiritual wickedness in high places (Eph. 6:12).

Do you understand what these things are? They are classes of demonic forces. Principalities and powers are a lower class of demons. Rulers of darkness are ranking demons. Spiritual wickedness in high places—they are the lieutenants of the demonic world. You need to understand that you're not fighting against flesh and blood; you're fighting against the spiritually wicked forces operating through flesh and blood, or through people.

Let's say that Mr. Brown has a ruler of the darkness inside him, and he keeps coming against you. How do you handle it? In prayer. That's where you are to do all your wrestling. You go to God in prayer and say, "God, in the name of Jesus, according to Your Word, I don't fight against flesh and blood, but against principalities, powers, and rulers of darkness in high places. I bind the spirit that operates in him, and I command it to cease in its maneuvers against me now, in the name of Jesus. I pray that the love of God and the communion of the Holy Spirit will begin to minister to Mr. Brown where I'm concerned."

First of all, you bind the spirit because the Bible says you must bind the strong man and then you'll be able to spoil his house—the strong man being the demonic force (Matt. 12:29). Don't forget to do that. Don't be at all surprised when you go to work the next day and Mr. Brown passes you, says hello, and even asks how you're doing. He was delivered during your intercessory prayer time.

That's the only way to handle this situation. You must look not at the flesh-and-blood person, but at the spirit operating through that person. I know what you're thinking. You're saying it's not a spirit; the person is just acting ugly. Believe me when I tell you, you're dealing with a spirit.

There is a definite relationship between wrestling against demonic forces and praying in tongues. In 1 Corinthians 14:2 we read, "For he that speaketh in an unknown tongue." Unknown to you, but not unknown. Someone, somewhere knows the tongue you speak in. I was prophesying once, and a gentleman in the congregation spoke the language that I was speaking. He interpreted silently as I began to give the group the interpretation of what I had said. He told my mother that he spoke the language I prophesied in and that I interpreted every word exactly. A spiritual gift and anointing operate through the interpretation, but they are unknown to the one speaking.

When you pray in tongues, you're not talking to the devil! You're talking to God about what the demons are doing. You're talking the Word of God and the will of God. God can easily take care of the devil.

God said that He created the smith that blows the coals in the fire (Isa. 54:16) and that no weapon formed against you shall prosper (Isa. 54:17). What does that mean to you? It means that He created the workman who forms weapons against you, and that you are not to concern yourself because He can handle him. His sin is none of your business. You're talking to God when you're talking in tongues. When you prophesy in a language that you interpret later, then you are talking to man.

I mentioned elsewhere that we have a church corporate prayer time on Saturday and before every service. Well, I didn't mention that the sessions are conducted in tongues.

Some people tell us that our Saturday morning prayer time is wrong and the church is out of order for conducting it. They say that because we all pray collectively in tongues.

"You know," they say, "the Bible says you ought not to pray in tongues without an interpretation" (1 Cor. 14:15). That rule applies only when you give a prophetic message to someone. But when we talk in tongues during corporate prayer, we're not talking to man; we're not talking to the devil; we're talking to God.

During that time, God takes advantage of using all those people who come together and pray at one time. He has intercession coming out of this mouth taking care of one situation and intercession all over the place taking care of all sorts of things. He sees our corporate prayer time as a smorgasbord of intercessors through which He can handle things all over the world.

On the other hand, if I prophesy in tongues before the congregation while everyone else is quiet, the Bible commands that I follow up with an interpretation. Otherwise, no one is edified with what came out of my mouth. When you fail to interpret a prophecy, people leave with their own private interpretations, and that causes conflict and confusion.

That's what Paul meant when he said in 1 Corinthians 14:19 that he would rather speak five words with understanding so that people could hear, understand, and be edified than to speak in tongues. He wasn't putting tongues down. He was saying that when it comes to preaching to men, he would rather be understood than speak in a language that people won't understand.

As for wrestling against the devil, well, he has already been defeated. You know that, don't you? We're not trying to defeat him. When we pray in tongues, we speak to God.

What I'm about to tell you should truly bless your heart. What follows is a familiar verse that will illustrate how this operates: "Likewise the Spirit also helpeth our infirmities" (Rom. 8:26). The Spirit here is capitalized because it refers to the Holy Spirit. The Holy Spirit will help you with the weaknesses of your flesh.

Is there any weakness that Paul was specifically zeroing in on? "For we know not what we should pray for as we ought" (Rom. 8:26). Bingo! There is the weakness. The weakness of prayer is that if you pray just in English, you pray only about the things of which you have knowledge. You pray only what you know about. What you don't know can hurt someone else because you can't pray for things you don't know about in your native language. Your prayer with understanding in your native language can fall short here.

Suppose your child is spending the summer with a relative.

This child is active and curious like most children and gets in a situation where he is about to be hit by a car. Your prayer would work if you had known beforehand that it was going to happen, but you didn't. What do you do? Could this be the weakness of prayer to which He referred?

Your flesh doesn't have the ability to know what's going on elsewhere unless someone else tells you. The Holy Spirit must help you out in this situation: "But the Spirit itself maketh intercession" (Rom. 8:26).

The Spirit Himself is getting ready to pray for and make intercession for someone else in your stead. But how? "With groanings which cannot be uttered" (Rom. 8:26). You know exactly what Paul was talking about. Go ahead. You can say it. He was talking about speaking in tongues! The Amplified Bible says, "And groanings too deep for utterance." The Spirit will pray *for* us, but He needs to do it *through* us.

He'll make intercession in places where we can't make it and for people we don't know we need to make it for, but He has to do it through us. I'm going to say this again, so pay attention. Who is going to pray for you? Your kid is somewhere about to be hit by a car, and Jesus says, "I'll intercede for you if you'll let Me intercede through you." He says, "I've got the prayer, and I can pray the prayer for you, but I'm not on the earth. I need a body, vocal cords, and a voice on the earth." Will you open your mouth and pray in groanings? Will you open your mouth and begin to speak in tongues? Who is talking is not important, but what's being said is supernatural and will take care of any situation.

Can you see what the devil has been doing to the church all this time? Here you are talking about how you're never going to speak in tongues, and the devil is having a field day. You may have refused to receive this gift from God because you were told that it's only for certain people. God is not a respecter of persons. He is not going to give one person the ability to pray, build up his life, and intercede for others and then withhold it from you.

When you don't receive, you are not giving God an avenue by which He can pray for you and eliminate that weakness of the flesh. Some preacher told you that speaking in tongues passed away with the last apostle. Somebody told you that you don't need to speak in tongues to get into heaven, so you didn't bother to take it any farther.

I never said that speaking in tongues is a requirement for entrance to heaven. On the contrary, speaking in tongues allows your prayers to be answered so that you might have heaven right here while you're on earth. Imagine, though, how you'll feel when you get to heaven and find out all the things that could have happened if you had let Jesus work through you.

Some people refuse to come to our church because we talk in tongues. It might seem like just a bunch of babbling to someone without knowledge of how God uses tongues, but you should see our results: families are prospering and disasters are averted. Here's what I like most about tongues. When Jesus is praying for you, everything has to obey. Everything!

You don't even have to set your alarm clock to get up to pray. God will wake you up during the night to use your vocal cords.

When the Spirit is praying through you, no prayer rules will ever be broken: "And he that searcheth the hearts knoweth what is the mind of the Spirit, because he maketh intercession for the saints according to the will of God" (Rom. 8:27). He will pray according to the will or the Word of God. The Holy Spirit knows everything and is everywhere at the same time. Wherever a family member may be, the Holy Spirit knows where the person is and what he or she is doing, what you're doing, and what everybody else is doing. That's how Jesus is able to forever make intercession for us. When He sees something going on in Russia that needs intercession, He wakes somebody up. And when He wakes you up, don't ask Him why He woke you; just pray. Anytime you are awakened to pray, do it. You don't know what could be happening. Pray! You don't necessarily have to get out of bed. You can pray where you are. Has that ever happened to you, and you didn't pray?

He is not going to let you go back to sleep. This is not the time to pop in a video. God needs your vocal cords. He needs to intercede in a way that you can't on your own. He needs someone to yield the tongue.

If you pray in tongues and don't understand what you say, all you have to do is to ask: "You do not have because you do not ask" (James 4:2 NKJV). If you don't understand, you obviously didn't ask Him. He says for you to pray that you might interpret. He'll tell you. Every now and then He'll let you in on what you've been praying: "And we know that all things work together for good" (Rom. 8:28).

Boy, have we butchered that particular verse. See what we've done? We started off in verse 26 talking about intercessory prayer, right? Verse 27 starts with *and,* indicating that we are connecting the thoughts of verse 26 with verse 27 and not yet finished with the subject of God's making intercession for us. Then verse 28 starts with another conjunctive word, indicating that we are to carry on from the thought from the previous verses: "And we know that all things work together for good to them that love God, to them who are the called according to his purpose" (Rom. 8:28).

What have you been saying that verse meant over the years? When a family member has a car wreck, some person who thinks he understands God stands up and says, "Well, remember, all things work together for the good of those who love the Lord." Have you ever heard anyone say that before?

"The reason you got leukemia is that God is trying to work something out in you. He is trying to test you. But remember, all things—even leukemia—work together for the good."

Tell me somebody, please, how is leukemia working for your good? The little kid who died in the car accident—how is that working for the good? Your house burned to the ground and you have nowhere to stay. Losing dear, precious relatives in tragic situations or being fired from your job and having no money and no seed to sow? How do these things work for the good? If you know, please tell me. You can't tell me because they don't.

"Well, you see, Pastor, if I was never fired from the job, then I would never have gotten this new job." Wrong. You would have gotten the new job if that's what God meant for you to have. He doesn't have to bring tragedy in order for you to see His purpose.

That's not what He is talking about here. He is talking about intercessory prayer and all the aspects of prayer, such as groanings in the Spirit and the assistance of the Holy Spirit. Those things working together in intercession work together for the good of those who will allow Jesus to intercede for them.

Through groanings, Jesus makes intercession for you. Every time you pray in tongues, anything that concerns you is being taken care of because Jesus is praying and He knows everything. And His intercession goes far beyond your ability to intercede. Boy, that's good news.

Don't misunderstand me, folks. God can take a terrible situation and turn it around and make something good happen. Just look in the mirror at yourself. Remember how you used to be and what God has done for your life. God majors in taking a mess and making a masterpiece out of it. But don't use that verse to prove that because it's the wrong one. Here He is talking about the love of God, yielding to the Holy Spirit, and praying in tongues so that you can get to where you've been called, according to His purpose. For years we've taken that out of context and confused people to the point that they thank God for car wrecks.

The Bible doesn't say to thank Him *for* everything. Before you start protesting, let me explain. It says to thank Him *in* everything. In other words, in the midst of a hard time, give thanksgiving to God—not for what happened, but for being God and for being your way out of whatever situation you find yourself in.

Don't be afraid to talk in tongues. Some people believe that once you start, it can't be controlled. Of course, you can control your tongue, your body, your emotions, and everything else about you. The Bible says that the spirit of the prophet is subject to the prophet (1 Cor. 14:32). You can even control your spirit. Anything God gives you can be controlled.

Intercession gives birth to the things we find ourselves experiencing. Through intercession, God brings to pass what an intercessor plants in prayer. Then He turns around and does something for you because you were the instrument that conceived a blessing in someone else's life. He couldn't have blessed that person without first having an intercessor to give spiritual birth through prayer.

Personally, I think it's awesome and count it a great privilege to be able to intercede for others. Those of you who pray in tongues have no idea of the wonderful things you've birthed in the spirit realm, and you won't know until you reach heaven. You might even find out that your prayers were responsible for great revivals of faith. I believe with all my heart that God will honor

those who, through the mercy and compassion of their intercession, brought about such things.

To pray in tongues is to pray the perfect prayer. When you
refuse to speak in tongues, you deny Jesus an avenue of intercession. You deny Him the opportunity to intercede through you on
behalf of others. I encourage everyone to be filled with the Holy
Spirit and have the evidence of speaking in tongues. To do so will
amplify the abundance and prosperity in your life because you're
able to pray about things you would not have been able to pray
for in the natural.

When you finish praying in tongues, there seems to be a
sense of satisfaction, as if you've taken care of things in God's
presence. Sometimes when you pray in your native language, you
feel as though you've left something out. When I pray in tongues,
I usually pray until a certain peace comes over me. That's my
indication that all is well. But the only way you'll know about
what I'm saying is to experience it for yourself.

Read 1 Timothy 2:5 with me: "For there is one God, and one
mediator between God and men, the man Christ Jesus." Jesus has
bridged the gap between God and men. And through intercession, He can take your prayer and give it directly to the Father.
Then the Father gives the results of your prayers back to Jesus.

Right now, tomorrow, next week, and until He returns, Jesus
is making intercession for us: "Therefore He is also able to save
to the uttermost those who come to God through Him, since He
always lives to make intercession for them" (Heb. 7:25 NKJV). Can
you see what you've been cutting off by refusing to speak in
tongues? This is Jesus' occupation. Until He comes back, Jesus
makes intercession for the saints. He does this when we pray in
tongues and when we pray in the Holy Spirit about things of
which we have no knowledge.

The unselfish part about praying in tongues is that you know you're not praying for yourself because you don't even understand what you're saying. I realize it can be difficult at first to spend an hour praying in the Spirit if you don't even know that anything is being sent up for you. But don't let the devil trick you into thinking that you're being forgotten when you send up prayers in the Holy Spirit. On the contrary, you have allowed yourself to be used by Jesus.

Seedtime and harvest. He must have someone to plant intercession in the earth for the harvest to come up and affect the lives of those who need prayer. He won't forget your labor of love. He will reward you and perfect all that concerns you. He will withhold no good thing from those who assist Him in doing His job.

Even with all the scriptural evidence I've given you, I know that someone reading this book wants to argue about what he has traditionally heard concerning tongues: "Well, you know, Paul said it's better to say five words in English."

You can't get to where God wants you to be on this matter because you're still arguing the basics. The only reason you would rather pray in English as opposed to praying in tongues is that you don't understand. I don't mind laying this foundation for you because I know that you can't do something you don't understand. If you're going to get anything from the Word of God, you first must have understanding (Prov. 4:7).

"For he that speaketh in an unknown tongue speaketh not unto men, but unto God" (1 Cor. 14:2). *Unknown,* as you can see if you read the verse in your Bible, is italicized, which means it didn't appear in the original Greek text. It's not completely unknown. In the book of Acts, when they were filled with the Holy Spirit, some men heard the disciples speaking in their various languages and wondered how they were able to do that. So, it's unknown only to the person speaking it. More important, when you speak in tongues, you're speaking to God, and He understands: "For no man understandeth him; howbeit in the spirit he speaketh mysteries" (1 Cor. 14:2).

I like what the Lord has given me to share with you about this verse. It's awesome. When you speak in tongues, you're speaking answers for the very questions you have in your life. And at the same time, by praying for someone else, out of you comes the answer. You can be struggling with something and start praying in the Holy Spirit and the answer comes.

As I mentioned earlier in this chapter, if I prophesy to you in tongues, I am obligated to interpret what I've said: "But he that prophesieth speaketh unto men to edification, and exhortation, and comfort" (1 Cor. 14:3).

You're the one being built up while you're praying in tongues: "He that speaketh in an unknown tongue edifieth himself" (1 Cor. 14:4). Try it. Whenever you're tired, depressed, or having a little pity party, try praying in tongues. You will come out with some pep in your step. It beats spending money for a psychologist.

A man who speaks in tongues edifies himself: "But he that prophesieth edifieth the church" (1 Cor. 14:4). Here is where the big dilemma comes in: "I would that ye all spake with tongues, but rather that ye prophesied: for greater is he that prophesieth than he that speaketh with tongues, except he interpret, that the church may receive edifying" (1 Cor. 14:5).

What was Paul saying? Prophesying in the language that the church speaks and understands is greater than speaking in tongues to the church except when you speak in tongues and interpret—then it's on the same level.

What was his concern? That when you speak to the church,

the people understand. He didn't say prophecy was greater than tongues. He said when you're addressing an assembly or speaking to someone, it's greater to speak in a language they understand than in a language they can't understand. But if you do speak in a language they don't understand and you give an interpretation, then that's all right. Why? Because you have achieved understanding in both situations, which is the ultimate goal.

> Now, brethren, if I come unto you speaking with tongues, what shall I profit you, except I shall speak to you either by revelation, or by knowledge, or by prophesying, or by doctrine? And even things without life giving sound, whether pipe or harp, except they give a distinction in the sounds, how shall it be known what is piped or harped? (1 Cor. 14:6–7)

You see, if you played these instruments and they all sounded like horns, how would you know which one was a piano or which was an organ unless each one had a distinct sound?

> So likewise ye, except ye utter by the tongue words easy to be understood, how shall it be known what is spoken? for ye shall speak into the air. There are, it may be, so many kinds of voices in the world, and none of them is without signification. Therefore if I know not the meaning of the voice, I shall be unto him that speaketh a barbarian, and he that speaketh shall be a barbarian unto me. (1 Cor. 14:9–11)

The bottom line is understanding. Paul said, "If I don't understand what he is saying, he is a barbarian to me."

Paul wrote, "Even so ye, forasmuch as ye are zealous of spiritual gifts, seek that ye may excel to the edifying of the church"

(1 Cor. 14:12). You might really be excited about spiritual gifts, but don't become so spiritual that you forget to edify the church. No one will be blessed if you don't understand what you're doing.

When you pray in tongues, ask God to give you the interpretation of what you prayed: "Wherefore let him that speaketh in an unknown tongue pray that he may interpret" (1 Cor. 14:13). When the interpretation comes, it will be revelation you can deposit in your understanding compartment for future reference.

I believe that when I pray in the Spirit before I preach, I'm actually rehearsing in tongues what will eventually come out in English. That's why I'm able to flow in such strong revelation knowledge when I pray because I've already spent time in the Holy Spirit. I've pulled up those mysteries, and they pop into my head and out of my mouth while I'm preaching. Again, I repeat, you have not because you ask not, so ask God for the interpretation.

Paul added, "For if I pray in an unknown tongue, my spirit prayeth, but my understanding is unfruitful" (1 Cor. 14:14). When you pray in tongues, your born-again spirit is praying, but your mind doesn't understand what's going on.

Paul continued, "What is it then? I will pray with the spirit" (1 Cor. 14:15). He was talking about praying in other tongues. "And I will pray with the understanding also" (1 Cor. 14:15). This, of course, means praying in English or whatever your native tongue happens to be. "I will sing with the spirit" (1 Cor. 14:15). Did you know that you can also sing in tongues? "I will sing with the understanding also" (1 Cor. 14:15).

When you pray in the Spirit, you don't understand, but when you pray in what the Bible calls the "understanding," you do. The limitation, however, is that you can pray only about what you have knowledge of. In tongues, you don't have to understand where, when, what, why, or how something is going on. You just pray and things are supernaturally taken care of.

If I should get up and start preaching in tongues, no one would be blessed by it but me because nobody can say amen to something he does not understand: "Else when thou shalt bless with the spirit, how shall he that occupieth the room of the unlearned say Amen?" (1 Cor. 14:16).

Paul declared, "For thou verily givest thanks well, but the other is not edified. I thank my God, I speak with tongues more than ye all: yet in the church I had rather speak five words with my understanding, that by my voice I might teach others also, than ten thousand words in an unknown tongue" (1 Cor. 14:17–19).

Do you see what Paul was saying in this passage? He was saying, "In the church, I would rather speak a language the people will understand than speak ten thousand words in a language they don't understand." Clearly, he was not putting down tongues or suggesting that they shouldn't be used. Paul was after what I am after, and that is for you to understand what is being said in church so that you can go home and do what the Word says to do. Some preachers can preach in English, and it still sounds like tongues because you don't understand a word they said.

> Brethren, be not children in understanding: howbeit in malice be ye children, but in understanding be men. In the law it is written, With men of other tongues and other lips will I speak unto this people; and yet for all that will they not hear me, saith the Lord. Wherefore tongues are for a sign, not to them that believe, but to them that believe not: but prophesying serveth not for them that believe not, but for them which believe. (1 Cor. 14:20–22)

If any man speak in an unknown tongue, let it be by two, or at the most by three, and that by course; and let one interpret. (1 Cor. 14:27)

We've not seen much of this in our church, but I'm believing that one day we will see more of this. Let's say the Spirit of God begins to move in the congregation, and there is a message in tongues. The Bible says to let him give that message and then be quiet. No one is to give another message by the Spirit until we get an interpretation of the first one. In this instance, the person was prophesying in church—not talking to God, but talking to the congregation. Then one or two more people may give Spirit messages, but no more than three, each with an interpretation before another one is heard. The head of the local church then has to determine whether or not the message is to be received.

The person who got up to speak may have spoken something that is out of perspective for that particular church and that time. So, it will be the responsibility of the leader of the church to judge what was spoken to determine if it was timely and in order for that church.

God is not the "author of confusion" (1 Cor. 14:33), and you may have been confused about speaking in tongues because the devil knows the effectiveness of this type of prayer.

No matter what you've heard, the devil cannot interpret what you pray in the Spirit, and it is definitely not a demonic language. Don't concern yourself with the notion that you might say something ugly while you're speaking in tongues because that can't happen. The Bible gives us peace about that: "Therefore I want you to understand that no one speaking under the power and influence of the (Holy) Spirit of God [ever] can say, Jesus be cursed! And no one can [really] say, Jesus is [my] Lord, except by and under the power and influence of the Holy Spirit" (1 Cor. 12:3 AMPLIFIED). My prayer is that I have cleared up your misconceptions about praying in the Spirit and that you will receive it freely as the gift God has given to all of His children.

Before you can effectively, successfully intercede for others, you need to address some areas in your life. Specific ingredients go into making a successful intercessor. They include the following:

1. *Agape* (pronounced ah-gah´-pay) love. You need to have love for people and want to see them delivered, set free, and saved. Don't become so spiritual that you are no earthly good to others. Don't consider yourself flawless or in a position to look down on others when they miss the mark. Love people so much that you pray constantly for them. You can't be an effective intercessor if you don't love others.

2. *Knowledge of the Word.* To pray effectively, you need to know who you are in Christ. You need to know your abilities, rights, and authority in the Anointed One and His anointing. If interceding for others is something you want to do, get into the Word as often as you can.

3. *Willingness to do the work.* It's not just loving people and knowing the Word; you must be willing to do what is necessary.

4. *Fervency.* James 5:16 states that "the effectual fervent prayer of a righteous man availeth much." Don't have a lackadaisical attitude about what you're doing for others. You must mean business when you pray.

5. *Awareness.* To be a good intercessor, you must be sensitive to the needs of others. Look beyond the person and into the spirit. God will sensitize you to pray for specific people. A person can be smiling on the outside and crying on the inside. God will let you know who needs prayer.

6. *Availability.* Are you available for God to use you? Are you willing to bear the hurt and pain of others? If God brought to mind a person for whom you are to pray, would you take the time to pray? The world looks for ability. God looks for availability. He has all the ability you need.

7. *Advocate.* An advocate represents another person and pleads his case or his cause. To be an advocate, you must plead with God on behalf of someone else. When you do that, you act more like Jesus than at any other time because He is the One who pleads our case.

8. *Acceptance.* God will place someone on your heart that you don't even like. Are you willing to accept the task of praying for someone you don't like? The quickest way to rid yourself of unforgiveness is to pray for that person. God has put on my heart to pray for people of whom I am not fond. I love them, but they are not my choices for daily fellowship. Often, when you start to pray for that person, you will find that he is not as much the problem as you are. God can show you more about yourself than the person He has assigned you to pray for.

9. *Abandonment.* Abandon all self-interest in the person for whom you are praying. Sometimes it's better for me to get someone else to pray for family members because I may have selfish motives invested in prayers that I would send up for them.

10. *Agonizing.* Be willing to bear the hurt of others. Be willing to pray for people in situations where you feel things just the way they feel them.

11. *Authority.* Understand your authority as an intercessor. Understand the promises of God. Some prayer sounds like begging because of sin. Read Luke 11:9: "Ask, and it shall be given." It doesn't say anything about begging. When a person doesn't

have confidence in the authority given him by the Word, he'll ask someone else to pray for him.

12. *The armor of God.* There is no armor designed for the back because we don't retreat; we take on the devil. Our breastplate and our shield are the Word of God. Take the Word of God to the devil in Jesus' name, and watch him retreat!

13. *Accountability.* If God places someone on your heart to pray for, you will be held accountable for your failure or faithfulness in so doing. This is not something you do at your convenience. God may wake you up at 2:00 A.M. to pray for someone. I can't tell you how miserable it will make you to be awakened by God to pray for someone, but you don't do it, and a tragedy occurs. On the other hand, it's a wonderful experience to pray for someone when God calls you to pray and then learn that the person was delivered from harm or tragedy. Don't worry about sleeping. God will redeem your time if you'll get up and pray in the Holy Spirit when He calls you.

Intercession is a major component of prosperity. Whatever you want to happen for you, make it happen for someone else through prayer. You do for others, and God will do for you.

If you don't speak in tongues and you want this gift, you first must be saved. Steps to salvation and steps to receiving the Holy Spirit with the evidence of speaking in tongues have been provided in the appendixes.

CONCLUSION

~~~

Our heart is not turned back, neither have our steps declined from thy way.

<div align="right">(Ps. 44:18)</div>

Prosperity is not limited to being blessed with having money at your disposal. Prosperity includes the ability to bless others with the love of God in your heart. It's having enough compassion, patience, love, and resources to meet not only your needs, but also the needs of someone else.

True prosperity is measured not by what you take out of the bank, but by what you take out of the Book and how you use what you've received to benefit mankind. It's having wealth, health, and the wisdom to do as God commands.

The Word of God is our instruction manual on how we are to pray for, receive, and distribute the blessings of God to make a mark in the lives of others that cannot be erased.

But, child of God, prosperity will cost you something.

In this book we've discussed the 14 steps to biblical prosperity:

Step 1: Ensure that the Lord is with you.

Step 2: Know God's ways and how He operates.

Step 3: Renew your mind with the Word of God on prosperity.

Step 4: Release words out of your mouth to establish your prosperity.

Step 5: Meditate upon the Word.

Step 6: Begin the process of seedtime and harvest.

Step 7: Stay consistent and committed to what you've planted.

Step 8: Recognize the difference between multiplied seed and harvest.

Step 9: Act as if it's so.

Step 10: Obey God's Word.

Step 11: Believe and trust in your man of God.

Step 12: Diligently seek and practice the presence of God.

Step 13: Quickly repent when necessary.

Step 14: Learn how to intercede.

Prosperity is not for a limited few, but for whosoever will take the steps ordered by God and follow them to the end: "For to this you were called, because Christ also suffered for us, leaving us an example, that you should follow His steps" (1 Peter 2:21 NKJV).

SALVATION

─❦─

Salvation is deliverance from the power and effects of sin. It is the state of breaking the authority of Satan over your life and allowing the light of Christ, the Anointed One, to empower you through righteousness. It's the process of exchanging the thoughts, words, and deeds of the world for the renewal of life found in the Word of God. Simply put, it's the road out of hell and the pathway into heaven.

1. *Admit/recognize that you are a sinner.* We all are born sinners, the result of Adam and Eve's transgression in the Garden of Eden. Stealing, lying, murder, and fornication are the fruit of sin and not what classify you as a sinner. Knowing this is the first step toward salvation.

2. *Repent.* To repent means to change your mind, to change your heart, and to change your direction. If you are now facing a life of sin, make a 180-degree turn away from darkness and into the marvelous light. Step out of the world and into the Word. To repent means more than to be sorry. It means to set yourself apart from the things you used to do. It means to walk away from your former activities. If at first you don't succeed, go to God, ask

for forgiveness, and repent again. The process of salvation is not complete until repentance takes place.

3. *Confess.* Your heart and your mouth must work together to bring your salvation to pass (Rom. 10:9–10). Words are spiritual containers that bring life to the process of salvation. Your confession must be that Jesus is Lord, and He sits on the throne of your life. The following prayer, spoken in an attitude of submission to God, will solidify the steps you have taken so far:

"Father, in the name of Jesus, I confess right now, and I realize that I am a sinner. I repent of all my sins. I make a 180-degree turn away from all my sins. I change my heart, I change my mind, I change my direction, and I turn toward Jesus Christ. I confess with my mouth that God raised Jesus from the dead, and I believe with my heart that Jesus is alive and operates in my life. I thank You, Lord, that I am saved. Amen."

4. *Experience water and Holy Spirit baptisms.* This is one step, but it involves two activities. Both are outward manifestations of salvation. The first one is natural, and the second is spiritual. Anyone who is saved should receive water baptism as a symbolic representation of the death, burial, and resurrection of Christ.

The second baptism is the baptism of the Holy Spirit with the evidence of speaking in tongues. You have to realize that God gave this gift to all of His born-again children on the day of pentecost. The Holy Spirit is already here. There is no need to wait, and there is no need to beg. Gifts, as you know, are freely given. The only thing you must do for this gift is to receive it. The only qualification for receiving this gift is that you must be born again. Although it is scriptural to have hands laid on you as a point of contact and support for this new activity, it is not necessary. It's mainly an act of releasing one born-again Christian's faith with another's. To begin speaking in tongues, you must open your mouth and speak in anything but your natural language.

What you hear at first may sound like babbling to you, but let it flow. The Holy Spirit acts on your vocal cords, lips, and tongue for the supernatural words to come out of your mouth, but you do the speaking. That's known as yielding to the Spirit. The sounds that come out will be spiritual and in no way demonic, as some people have been deceived into believing. Speaking in tongues is actual cooperation between you and the Holy Spirit.

5. *Obey God's Word.* Confessing Jesus Christ as your Lord and personal Savior is just the beginning. As a born-again, Spirit-filled Christian, you must obey the Word of God. However, you can't obey the Word if you don't know the Word. The only way for you to live a successful life as a Christian is to stay in constant fellowship with the Father. Read your Bible daily, pray, exercise your faith, and allow yourself to grow in the things of God. If you do not presently belong to a Bible-teaching, faith-believing, Spirit-filled, Word-based church, pray and ask God to lead you to such a church that you may grow spiritually.

Complete salvation, or *soteria* as it is called in the Greek translation, includes your health, wealth, soundness, protection, and deliverance from every curse, including death. Because we are children of the King, death has no victory over us because we will live eternally with the Anointed One.

RECEIVING THE HOLY SPIRIT

1. Understand that the Holy Spirit was poured out on the day of pentecost (Acts 2:38).
2. Realize that salvation is the only qualification necessary for receiving the Holy Spirit baptism (Acts 2:38).
3. Laying on hands is scriptural (Acts 8:17).
4. For an explanation of what to expect when you speak in tongues read Acts 19:6.
5. Disregard all fears about receiving a counterfeit language (Luke 11:11–13).
6. Open your mouth as an act of faith (Eph. 5:18–19).
7. Let all things be done decently and in order (1 Cor. 14:33).

ABOUT THE AUTHOR

CREFLO A. DOLLAR JR. was born and raised in College Park, Georgia. After graduating from Lakeshore High School, he obtained a Bachelor of Education degree with a concentration in history from West Georgia College in Carrollton, Georgia.

He began his professional career as a high school teacher in the Fulton County school system. From there, he became an educational therapist for Brawner Psychiatric Institute of Atlanta.

In 1986, Creflo Dollar began to carry out the call God had placed on his life by starting World Changers Christian Center, a nondenominational church in College Park. He began the ministry at a local elementary school with only eight people. At that time, the ministry was small and aimed at developing a solid foundation for the fulfillment of a larger vision.

He now pastors a church of more than seventeen thousand members, and he is an internationally known author, teacher, and conference speaker with a ministry that reaches beyond the local community to countries throughout the world. He can be seen and heard on the *Changing Your World* broadcast, via television and radio, and in meetings and conventions worldwide.

He and his wife, Taffi, live in Atlanta. They have five children—Gregory, Jeremy, Jordan, Alexandria, and Lauren Grace.

OTHER BOOKS AND TAPES BY CREFLO A. DOLLAR JR.

≈

BOOKS

Attitudes

Capturing the Reality of Heaven and Hell

Confidence: The Missing Substance of Faith

The Anointing to Live

The Color of Love

The Divine Order of Faith

The Sins of the Mouth

Understanding God's Purpose for the Anointing

TAPE SERIES

1997 Faith Convention: The True Source of Power

And Jesus Healed Them All

Christ in You: The Hope of Glory

Communication: The Master Key to an Anointed Family

Printed in the United States
36750LVS00002B/52